# *Conversations with an Unbelieving Friend*

John Carmody

PAULIST PRESS
New York/Mahwah

Library of Congress Cataloging-in-Publication Data

Carmody, John, 1939–
    Conversations with an unbelieving friend/ by John Carmody.
      p.  cm.
    ISBN 0-8091-3210-9
    1. Catholic Church—Apologetic works.  2. Apologetics—20th century.  3. Imaginary conversations.  I. Title.
    BX1752.C28   1990
    239—dc20
                                        90-47787
                                         CIP

Published by Paulist Press
997 Macarthur Boulevard
Mahwah, New Jersey 07430

Printed and bound in the
United States of America

# Contents

ॐ

*For Grace Mojtabai,*

*a Friend I Believe*

# Preface

ॐ

This book is a work of fiction. There is no unbelieving Deborah in my real world. On the other hand, I have many secular friends who seem to consider Christian faith irrelevant. Thinking about them, I have conceived a conversation in which to take up the challenges in their unbelief. Although some of these challenges are daunting, at the end I have been more impressed by the deep solutions the gospel carries, when one lets it engage with the rawest human needs.

I owe thanks to Larry Boadt, my editor, and to Kevin Lynch, my publisher, for making Paulist Press so welcoming to creative ventures. I also owe thanks, as always, to my wife Denise, for stimulus and support. Readers who want a better book on faith, certainly one more artful, should take up A.G. Mojtabai's *Ordinary Time* (Doubleday, 1989).

# 1

# *Is Religion Necessary?*

*John:* "I've been wanting to discuss something with you. The other day, when we got into the question of what makes a sane lifestyle, you balked at the notion of meditation or prayer. Exercise, work, friendship, relaxation, and the other things we mentioned were fine. But you said, almost aggressively, 'I don't pray or meditate.' Why was that?"

*Deborah:* "I'm not sure. I guess the idea makes me nervous. I'm a quite secular person. My parents were not religious. I don't know much about meditation or prayer. And, to be honest, I don't feel the need. To whom would I pray? What benefit would meditation bring?"

*John:* "You would pray to God. Meditation probably would alleviate some of your nervousness, help you get off that emotional roller-coaster you ride so often."

*Deborah:* "Ouch. That's direct. Do you think I'm unstable?"

*John:* "Debbie, Debbie. What do we talk about week after

week? We talk about one little crisis after another. Your mind is sharp as a knife. But more times than not it's dulled by worry. You laugh about that yourself. But I sometimes think you've come to enjoy crisis, or at least to expect it. It's as though you've decided that a full life means always feeling something intensely—as though you get bored when things unfold smoothly, undramatically."

*Deborah:* "That's not fair. Most of the crises are not my fault, and I certainly don't enjoy them. Do you think the pains in my back are psychosomatic, or the fights with Renée are fun, or I'm making up the stupidity of my boss?"

*John:* "Easy. I'm not accusing you. I'm trying to get your attention so that we can talk about things more realistically. You claim that you're on the edge, that you're not happy, that you wish you had more control. Yet we both know that you've been speaking this way for years. There's a clear pattern to your swings of mood. Outsiders would say that you've got it together very well. You're good at your work, and you're charming on social occasions. But with your friends, the story is different. I know it's partly a matter of just letting off steam, the way we all do. But another part is debilitating, dysfunctional. If you could stop defending yourself for a moment, maybe we could clarify what creates that other part, those emotional excesses."

*Deborah:* "You're right. I am defensive. I went to a psychiatrist once, years ago, and it was not a good experience. I don't want to look carefully at my emotional swings, yet of course I'm obsessed with them. So I pour everything out to a few good friends—it's a lot cheaper than a psychiatrist. But I guess I forget that after a while those friends see patterns, and that I may be wearing out my welcome. Right now I feel like a little girl who cried wolf too often."

*John:* "Forget the past for a moment. Concentrate on what I'm asking right now. Why doesn't the idea of praying to God appeal to you? What turns you off or creates a problem?"

*Deborah:* "I don't know whether I believe in God. Maybe I do, but I'm not sure. And I'm also not sure what difference it would make if I did believe in God. God doesn't seem to play a strong role in the things that interest me. Except for you, most of my friends are not religious. I admire the calm that you project, but I'm not sure whether that comes from your dealings with God."

*John:* "And you're also not sure you want to be calm the way I am. You think it might take away much of the excitement or dull the edge."

*Deborah:* "To be honest, yes. I like my life, most of the time. I don't like the real lows, and sometimes I feel exhausted. But part of me is fascinated by the predicaments I get into. They may be trying, but they make me feel alive."

*John:* "What do you do with the excitement, the *joie de vivre,* that comes when you feel alive?"

*Deborah:* "What do you mean, what do I do with it?"

*John:* "I mean, do you come back to it in a reflective moment and say, 'Yes, that justifies the way I'm living, even justifies my life itself'? Do you send out a feeling of thanks or gratitude, perhaps unverbalized, for being in a world or a body or a personality that makes such excitement possible? Or does the excitement make little lasting impact, just fade away until the next occurrence?"

*Deborah:* "I don't know. I've never thought about it. I guess if you asked me what makes my life seem good, I would point to the excitement, the sense of being fully alive, charged with adrenaline. I guess I would say that the good times—when my work seems to make a difference, or I'm in love, or Renée and I have been close—make it all seem worthwhile. But I don't think much beyond that sort of justification. I'm not much of a metaphysician."

*John:* "Well, if you're really satisfied with your life, perhaps you don't have to be. Still, I'm surprised that you don't wonder more about what your insights, or the times when things fall into place, mean in bigger perspective. You strike me as too intelligent, and too well-educated, not to be curious about the overall scheme of things. Or have you decided that curiosity of that sort doesn't pay much of a dividend?"

*Deborah:* "Yes, I think I have decided that. The few times I've thought hard about the long view—God, or immortality, or a cosmic pattern—I haven't gotten very far. The data seem so confusing or mixed that I can't come to any clear conclusion. On the one hand, there are peak experiences that make me feel life is so beautiful that it has to have a transcendent meaning. On the other hand, the peak experiences are few, most days are unspectacular (even for a crisis-junkie like me), and sometimes, when I'm low, I think the universe is just a cruel joke. So I don't waste a lot of time on the big picture."

*John:* "My turn to say 'ouch.' It's painful to hear someone speak of thinking about the big picture as a waste of time. That's the only thing I really like to think about. It's the only thing that soothes my soul. I love to realize that nobody knows, with an empirical sort of certainty, how everything fits together. I'm delighted when it becomes clear that the past was as messy as the present is, or that my heroes had to worry about sickness, or problem children, or superiors who did not appreciate them."

*Deborah:* "Why does that sort of thing delight you? It would depress me."

*John:* "It delights me because it makes me think that it's right, necessary, healthy for us human beings not to know. It delights me because I take it to mean that God—someone who could know, someone who's not limited in all the ways we are—is natural or objective. At least in the mode of mysteriousness, God comes into view whenever I ask more than two questions in a row, along a logical line in search of explanation. And, somehow, contemplating this mysterious God feeds my spirit.

Without words, in simple recollection, it functions like sleep, knitting up the raveled sleeve of care. I suspect this is what yogins and shamans have experienced down the ages. There's a certain rightness, a certain liberation, that comes from contemplating the Whole, the All, the Foundation—call it whatever you will. I can't conceive of living without such contemplation. It would be like having a house with no windows, or like blocking out a wonderful skylight."

*Deborah:* "Are you leading me toward Plato's parable of the cave?"

*John:* "Good for you. I didn't have that in mind, but it's right on the mark. Yes, I believe that without contemplation I would be living in the dark, not even aware of how much I was missing. I believe that the purely physical life, or even the purely emotional life, doesn't come close to revealing our human potential."

*Deborah:* "But is there a purely physical life, or a purely emotional life? Don't we always mix in ideas, images, second thoughts?"

*John:* "We do indeed, yet contemplation shows our need to attend to movements in our spirits that take us beyond our debts to matter and matter's place in our inner life. But you've got to go. I'll see you soon."

§~

*John:* "Let me return to the matter of contemplation, because it's where I find the heart of religion. Other people might tell you that the heart of religion is practical love of one's neighbor. I wouldn't dispute them, but to my mind what makes such love, or anything else, religious is its connection with God. 'God' is the personal name I give to the mysteriousness toward which my mind and heart move when I step back to reflect or pray. Certainly I interpret this mysteriousness in virtue of my

Christian upbringing and faith. Certainly I could speak about it in trinitarian terms. But taken simply as a matter of common human experience, before one inserts heavy interpretation, 'God' appears to me as the Beginning or the Beyond or the Depth that my spirit seeks, whenever it yearns for rest and nourishment."

*Deborah:* "That's a novel way of putting it. I tend to seek rest and nourishment from other people. Sometimes I enjoy being alone, and sometimes my thoughts go toward the puzzle of things, the fact that I seem in over my head. But I don't know how to linger with ideas like the Beginning or the Beyond. They're too abstract for me. How could they prove nourishing?"

*John:* "They're not abstract for me, though I don't really like them as names. They just specify, tie down slightly, the movement of my spirit toward explanation or satisfaction. The strange part of such movement is that nothing definite or particular can satisfy me. The movement goes beyond all particulars, toward something literally infinite. Sure, I've got to imagine God as a sort of ocean or limitless expanse of space or time. But that's not what nourishes my soul. What nourishes my soul is a darkness, an unformed presence, that isn't an idea or an image. It's like a companion of my mind and heart, a conspirator, in the root sense of something that breathes with me, that is spirit alongside me, supporting the outreach of my mind and heart. I don't know why it's nourishing to find this conspirator and abide with it, except that only dealing with such an unlimited, mysterious reality seems to fulfill the capacity at my core."

*Deborah:* "Is this some sort of mysticism?"

*John:* "At most a very tame one. I think that we can experience God, and I suppose that ultimately such experience is stimulated by God, inasmuch as God is the major partner in the relationship. If one uses the classical definition of mysticism, 'patiens divina' (experiencing divine things), then perhaps mine is a mystical experience. But it has none of the drama, and only a few of the harrowing and so purifying effects, that the great mystical authors speak about. It's a mysticism available to most people willing to reflect and be still. One could call it an habitual or acquired contemplation."

*Deborah:* "And what difference does it make in your life?"

*John:* "Not as much as it should, but still enough to make it precious. It gives me perspective. I'm less likely to construct the universe around my own ego. And it's a way to deal holistically with the fullness that my life, or any life, seems to entail. I can read Stephen Hawking about the wonders of the origin of the cosmos, or I can muse with Annie Dillard about the complexities of the biosphere, but I can only engage with the Whole, the Mystery, that such descriptions conjure up by stopping my mind and letting my spirit, my core self, wrap itself around God without words, or ideas, or even images."

*Deborah:* "And what makes this prayer? I thought prayer was asking God for the things we need."

*John:* "What makes this prayer is a decision to treat the Mystery one comes upon, the Whole to which one is trying to relate holistically, as venerable—something so good and holy that one wants one's wrap-around to be a form of worship, of love full of praise. My religious background makes me treat the Mystery as personal. So, on occasion, I also ask God for what I need, what I sense the world needs, what would make all of us better—less evil, more creative and truthful and good. Prayer is not limited to asking God for what we need, but unless we do ask God for what we need, we don't have a fully personal sense of God or kind of prayer. The core of prayer, most saints would say, is gratitude to God for God's own goodness. That's the root meaning of the word 'eucharist.' The best effects of contemplation in my life are results of such gratitude. At the moments when prayer seems to have worked best, I find my life a matter of pure grace. There was no necessity for me to be, let alone to have the chance to enjoy so many good things. It has all been grace, the pure effect of God's goodness."

*Deborah:* "But surely there have been bad things in your life—times of pain, or failure, or injustice? How can you consider them God's grace? Are we supposed to be grateful for our sufferings?"

*John:* "A tough question. I don't know how familiar you are with the Catholic liturgy for Easter, but during the Vigil there's a famous song, called the Exultet, that speaks of Adam's sin as a 'happy fault.' Now, Adam's sin is a code-word for the origin of everything wrong in the moral order. All of the social injustice, the bloodshed of warfare, the hurts and lusts and distortions that we can trace to human irrationality and selfishness are compressed into 'Adam's sin.' How could all of that be a happy fault, a cause for joy and praising God? Because it led to the demonstration of God's love that Christians find in the career of Christ. The apostle Paul said that where sin abounded, grace has abounded the more. The entire New Testament speaks of the message generated by Christ as a good news, a declaration that even when our hearts condemn us, God is greater than our hearts. So, in a strange way, all manner of thing finally is well, and one day it will be revealed that God has always been all in all. The Christian understanding of redemption is that God can turn evil into good. How God can do this, we don't understand. But that God can do this is a function of what we mean by 'God,' and of what God did with Christ's sufferings on the cross."

*Deborah:* "All of a sudden you've gotten very Christian. Are you saying that one has to be a Christian to understand that mystery you were saying you find in contemplation, or to believe that all of human life is grace and so something for which we should be grateful?"

*John:* "No, I'm not saying that. I think that any people who believe in God can find ways of reverencing the mystery, calling it divine, and making it the reason they consider their lives to be wonderful gifts. On the other hand, my biography has been Christian, so I tend to explicate the mystery in Christian terms, especially when it comes to the matter of everything that seems ungracious—ugly, evil, painful, something that should not be. The most powerful symbolism I know of for dealing with sin and grace is the career of Jesus of Nazareth, especially his crucifixion and resurrection. So, if you pushed me, I would finally say that my contemplation leads me to make the crucifixion and resurrection of Christ the context for interpreting any human pain, whether it be my regret that often I don't find God or don't serve God well, or your upset from physical pain, or problems at work, or difficulties with your daughter."

*Deborah:* "I took a course in art that included some famous depictions of the crucifixion. At first they put me off, but after a while I came to sense that many of the artists were trying to work out something universal—to make a statement about all human pain. I suppose I never took seriously the idea that the Son of God was dying on those crosses. But I was moved by the sufferings of the man Jesus, especially when I took him as an everyman. It was consoling, somehow, to think that suffering is what tends to happen if one speaks the truth or challenges the powers that be. But I suppose you would want to say more than that."

§∙

*John:* "I would, if the time were right. One day I'd like to discuss what Christians do, and don't, mean by the divinity of Christ. But right now I think it's more relevant to relate this issue of grace and suffering, good things and bad things, to the question with which we began, the utility of prayer. 'Utility' is not really a good word to use for prayer, since those who pray faithfully tell us that with time God tends to take center stage and our human notions of profit or gain tend to recede. Still, if there were no benefit in praying, most people would never get to the stage where they sometimes forget themselves and concentrate wholly on God. My proposal to you is that prayer can do good things for you, and included in that proposal is the wider notion that religion can do good things for you."

*Deborah:* "That raises a question about the relation between prayer and religion, but let me bracket that for a while. I've been listening to your descriptions of contemplation and grace, wondering why they sound more familiar than I would have expected. By using language that I find more philosophical or psychological than religious, you've made contemplation and grace less alien. I've read enough good literature to know that whenever writers want to describe moments of insight that change a character's life they edge toward religious language. They may not use the word 'conversion,' but they're in that psychic area. The most fascinating moments in any of the lives we observe, actual or literary, are the times when people come to themselves and realize, with a shock, that they've had things all wrong. Only in light of such times do people's ordinary ideas and actions become interesting: they might be moving toward a moment of insight, or they are expressing the self-knowledge that they have acquired to date."

*John:* "So you're saying that self-knowledge is a large part of what makes people interesting?"

*Deborah:* "Yes, I think I am. That was the advice of the oracle at Delphi, as you know very well, and I've always loved the probings of Socrates, and greatly respected the idea that he was the wisest man in Athens because he knew what he didn't know. No doubt you would like to quote me the parable about the prodigal son, the decisive moment of which the King James version describes in that language of coming to oneself that I used spontaneously. See, even an unreligious person like me has been influenced by biblical language! A few times I've come to myself, and I'm always hoping that I will have the experience again. For the light to dawn, the blinders to fall, things suddenly to come clear—that's a pearl of great price."

*John:* "If it's not too personal, tell me what you learned when you came to yourself."

*Deborah:* "It was personal, but the implications seemed to stretch far beyond just my own situation. Once, I realized that my marriage had become impossible. I guess I had known it subconsciously for several years and been unwilling to face up to it. Finally, after another terrible fight, I was walking by the river when it struck me that I could leave. I had imagined leaving, of course, but never as a realistic option. Renée was small and I wasn't sure I could get a job in another city. But at that moment by the river things turned over and leaving became realistic, even obvious. It was as though I'd finally shaken the kaleidoscope hard enough to create a pattern, a new scheme fitting all the pieces together. Part of me feared the idea of leaving, but another part shouted with joy. I felt released, liberated. I no longer had to conceive of my future as tied to David's whims. I could move out and start over. It was a wonderful feeling, and even though I knew that acting on it would not be easy, I felt as though I'd been given a second chance, had undergone a kind of rebirth."

*John:* "But you would not call that religious, or think that Socrates or the prodigal son was relevant?"

*Deborah:* "Well, I don't know. I guess I'd have to hedge. Certainly Socrates and the prodigal son were relevant, because they had contributed to my conviction that self-knowledge is crucial. I'd learned some things from the psychiatrist I was seeing, but I'd found that I learned more on my own, by simply sifting through my hopes and fears. On the other hand, I didn't have any vision of God. In fact, I probably thought that God could never approve of divorce. But I can see how you might call my experience religious, because it did take me out of myself and into the mysteriousness of our human condition. When I said that the implications of my insight stretched beyond myself, I meant that I got a strong appreciation of the strangeness of our minds and decisions. I wondered, even at the time, why things had become clear at just that moment. There was a lovely willow tree at a bend of the river diagonally across from me, and I remember weaving the graceful droop of that tree into my joy at feeling freed. Did the tree trigger something subliminally? And what would wave out from my new sense of freedom? How would my life, and Renée's, and even David's be changed, if I followed through? Perhaps because I was near water, I thought of the ripples a pebble makes when it drops into the water. As it turned out, my life did change significantly. I quit my job, moved, and began a new life in a new city. All because I came to myself one spring day by the river, across from a willow tree. If the mysteriousness of that experience matches up with what you mean by mysteriousness, then maybe we're not so far apart."

*John:* "It does indeed. And the religious word matching the kind of question or wonder you felt is 'providence.' Why do things happen in the world as they do? Is it all chance, or does everything comprise a gigantic quilt, a pattern so vast that only an infinite God could see it, yet so exact that every detail has its place? Religious people are moved toward abandoning themselves to divine providence. Bit by bit, the gravity of their faith takes them toward the realization that they will never understand the whole pattern of creation and so have to trust that it makes sense. Whom should they trust? Only the one who could know the full pattern and bear ultimate responsibility for it. The Bible says, 'Put not your trust in princes.' Why? Because princes are creatures of a day. The only proper, wise place to put one's trust is in someone who perdures, who is greater than all the contingencies we find in our experience, all the change and death. So, when we experience the mysteriousness of an insight or a decision, we have to wonder about the whole pattern into which it fits, and about what might secure either it or that whole pattern in meaning. What can we depend upon? That's the question that takes us into the aspect of the divine mystery called divine providence."

*Deborah:* "I used to think that I could rely on my family and friends. Then I thought that I could rely only on myself. Now you seem to be telling me that I can rely only on God, this mysteriousness that you keep bringing in. I'll have to think about that. Is it possible to live placing one's hopes in something one can't see or hear or speak to? That's a real stretch for a worldling like me. I like to eyeball the people I'm forced to trust. I like to keep close tabs on them."

*John:* "That's funny, because it makes me ask whether prayer is trying to eyeball God or keep tabs on divine providence. Maybe sometimes it is. We ask God to draw near, make himself (or herself) known, tell us what's going on or what we ought to do. And usually we get no answer, at least no indubitable answer. But often, I think, we come away changed, and so maybe we have received or produced an 'answer.' I find it can be an answer to realize again that there is often no answer—no clear imperative, no obvious explanation. If that is the nature of the world, the reality, in which I am involved, then I can stop seeking definitive solutions to my questions about peace, stability, order, how to ground a life in meaning—the questions I'm always raising. I can stop beating myself up for not having everything under control. To have everything under control, I would have to be God. Can I become God? Obviously not. Yet, so teasing is a religion such as Christianity, I can hope to become united with God, and so become part of what does have everything under control. It's almost amusing: there's no end to the possibilities, once one adopts a religious horizon and lets the mystery become the foremost reality."

§⌒

*Deborah:* "I don't want to mislead you. That time when I came to myself and settled the question of my divorce was far from typical. True, there have been a few other dramatic moments, when things fell into place and I got enough light to take some decisive steps, but I don't go looking for enlightenment. In fact, I may think that you can't go looking for enlightenment —that it has to happen spontaneously, when the pressure of your problems gets great enough to force you to create a new pathway."

*John:* "So you want to back away from the religion that I credited you with, on the basis of your sense of mystery that time by the river?"

*Deborah:* "No, not really. I just want to be honest about the way I usually act and feel, which I don't consider religious. Granted, the mysteriousness I experienced was intriguing, and probably part of my experience of liberation. Still, I haven't felt compelled to keep pondering that mysteriousness, let alone to pray to it. Perhaps I'd be a better person if I had, but the fact is that most days I'm preoccupied with quite practical problems."

*John:* "Yes, I understand. But I'm not sure that I agree. It seems to me that those practical problems often make you reflect on what sort of a person you are, or what you really want out of life, or where you're going to find the job or the personal relationship that gives you the fulfillment you're seeking—the fulfillment you haven't yet found. Now and then you've mentioned that kind of reflection to me, and I've inferred that it's a regular feature of your melancholy."

*Deborah:* "But even I don't take it fully seriously. Even I know it's a form of self-indulgence. I'm feeling sorry for myself so I dip into *Weltschmerz*."

*John:* "Yes, but is it only feeling sorry for yourself? Isn't there also an inchoate questioning about what sort of a world you live in—about what we can realistically expect, or hope for, or yearn to have happen?"

*Deborah:* "Maybe. But I'm not inclined much to abstractions. Most of my reflection is concrete: how did I mess things up? Why is this man making me miserable? How much should I worry about Renée's dating? What you call reflection and seem to want to make religious is more detached and far-ranging than I usually become."

*John:* "O.K. We can come back to that, because I only agree with you partially. I have another, similar question, though. When you are brooding about your problems, or examining your character for flaws, or cursing at the fates, do you ever agree to the longings that well up in you? Do you ever own up your deepest hungers and wants—things like the desire to be known and loved fully, completely, unconditionally? Or like the desire to stop running, get off the treadmill, fall into the arms of a rest and peace that would embrace you, like a mother taking her child to her bosom?"

*Deborah:* "I've never pictured my longings that way, but I have to admit that I've had them. On the other hand, I don't think I've considered them significant. Just because I'd like steak for dinner doesn't mean there's a steak in my freezer. Just because I want a perfect love or rest doesn't mean it's realistic to expect one. In fact, experience tells me it isn't realistic to expect one. Who has ever found that kind of love or fulfillment?"

*John:* "A good question, but I'm not sure how to answer it. The obvious answer is, 'No one.' But maybe that's not true. Many people report moments of perfect fulfillment, when they feel flooded with love, acceptance, and peace. Certainly, such moments are rare, occurring maybe two or three times in the

15

average person's lifetime. Still, they can be very significant, both for the people themselves, and for strange characters like me who think about their implications. Indeed, when it comes to the lives of the saints, or the people who make history, like a Martin Luther or a Mahatma Gandhi, moments of profound consolation, sometimes in counterpoint to moments of profound desolation seem frequent, almost expectable. Finally, I sometimes think that it's possible to speak of a diluted yet fairly constant, more-often-than-not, sort of consolation—a semi-habitual feeling of resting on the bosom of the divine mysteriousness."

*Deborah:* "You're losing me. I can picture what you're describing, but it's a very optimistic interpretation of an interior life like mine. A saint I am not. Can a neurotic be a saint? Don't answer that! I don't really think I'm a neurotic, but I am tossed up and down a lot. In fact, if I didn't function so well in my job, I might wonder seriously about my emotional stability. To date, I've been able to put off that kind of wondering by reasoning that if I'm able to put my personal worries aside when it is necessary to pay attention or make decisions in my job, I must be reasonably healthy. What do you think?"

*John:* "I think you're reasonably healthy, not the least because you have some perspective on your emotional swings. And, for the record, I do think that neurotics can be saints—the canon is full of them! Whether I'm being optimistic in thinking that a life such as yours can reveal a regular buoyancy is up to you to say. I only ask that you analyze more closely what it is that keeps you going—what in fact you rely upon, on the good days, which in your case outnumber the bad, at least insofar as your being able to function adequately means a good day. Let me complicate things further, though, by mentioning the experience that seems to have buoyed Jesus, through both good days and bad. For Jesus, apparently, the divine mystery was so personal and close that he could speak to it intimately, calling it his

'Abba' ('Father,' in a familiar sense). Moreover, he could rely on it absolutely, commending his spirit into its safekeeping. For a Christian trying to interpret the foundations of human perseverance, Jesus' trust is bound to be provocative. Perhaps the way for any of us to become free—and Jesus was nothing if not a free spirit—is to entrust ourselves to the divine mysteriousness the way that he did."

*Deborah:* "But look what it got him! Jesus ended up crucified—'despised, rejected, a man of sorrows, and acquainted with grief,' as Handel's *Messiah* puts it."

*John:* "Yes, that's what it got him. But only that? What about the resurrection of Jesus, which his earliest followers considered to be his Father's ratification of his message and person and so of his profound trust? What about the many indications that Jesus had peak moments when the lilies of the field, or small children, or the pain of a crippled person became revelations?"

*Deborah:* "Whoa! I'm not going to argue about Jesus with a theologian. Suffice it to say that I find the resurrection even more difficult than the crucifixion. Besides, what does either one of them have to do with my life, except as a dramatic symbol—a blow-up of the small dyings and risings we all experience?"

*John:* "Maybe, just maybe, the crucifixion and resurrection of Jesus, and many of the other symbols one finds in religion, clarify the experiences of quite ordinary people like you and me. Maybe we're all bound to be religious, in the sense of being involved with a mysteriousness clarified provocatively by holy people such as Jesus. Wouldn't that sizzle your steak: to be human you'd have to be involved with the stuff the religions make central. No, don't hit me. Be nice. I'm your friend, remember. Your obnoxious religious friend."

# 2

# Religion, or Ethics?

*Deborah:* "Let me ask you something. Why isn't it enough to concentrate on ethics? The people I admire are the people who do the right thing. They try to make a difference in the world. When it comes to the work they choose, or how they raise their kids, or the needs of their community, they support what is fair and make life better for everyone. If people's religion helps them to spend their time and money on good causes, fine and dandy. But if it does not, I have no respect for it."

*John:* "A fair enough question, though perhaps more complicated than it first seems. On the one hand, I can agree with you fully that what people do is the best criterion of their character. People who talk a good game but don't follow through are not to be trusted. There's a saying of Jesus to the effect that it's not those who say, 'Lord, Lord,' but those who do the Father's will, who enter the kingdom of heaven. The liberation theologians have given this teaching a sharp edge: only those who are struggling for justice understand what the gospel means. On the other hand, it's not easy to decide in all cases what the right, the just, the loving course of action is. People of good will can disagree legitimately. And, when one traces down

18

the roots of their disagreements, one can find different under-standings of human nature or human responsibility. Many times, such understandings are rooted in people's religious con-victions, whether expressed or tacit. So, many times religion does have a bearing on people's ethical outlook—not just whether or how they act, but what they think they ought to be doing."

*Deborah:* "May we make this more concrete? Take the six Jesuits slain in San Salvador in November of 1989. What made their deaths more significant than the deaths of any other peo-ple working for justice in Central America? I would say that it was what they were doing—standing up to that country's foul right wing, trying to raise political consciousness, educating lit-tle children for a decent future, pointing out the complicity of the United States in the murders of the army death squads, and the like—that made them heroes. Certainly, they drew their idealism from their religious convictions. But many other peo-ple share their political or cultural ideals, without sharing their Christian faith."

*John:* "Now there's a sad, sobering example. I would call those men martyrs, as well as heroes, because they were killed for their convictions, as well as for their actions. The right wing feared and hated their conception of the church, which stressed the priority of the needs of the poor over the wants of the wealthy. In a country with deep cultural roots in Catholicism, their view of the church, and so of society and culture, carried truly revolutionary potential. There's also the fact that they put themselves on the line for their view, not only through the modest political activity they carried out (Ellacuria's mediating the return of Duarte's kidnaped daughter, Martin-Baro's con-ducting opinion polls), but also through their whole lifestyle, which sought to identify them with El Salvador's poor. So, without denigrating the perhaps areligious convictions of others who have put themselves on the line in Central America or even been murdered, I tend to think that one can't separate religion and ethics, belief and political action, in the case of the six slain Jesuits."

*Deborah:* "O.K. I can follow your reasoning. But would you agree that the difference between those heroes or martyrs and the many other Christians in Central America who either support the right wing or try to stay out of the conflict is what the Jesuit six actually did?"

*John:* "Yes, with a couple of qualifications. First, there is the matter not only of what the six Jesuits actually did, but of what was done to them. They were singled out. Others might have been, but were not. Second, if those others thought the same way as the six Jesuits, and lived out their convictions (perhaps not so dramatically, but nonetheless really), then the difference between them (who were not killed) and the Jesuits would be mysterious—a matter of providence, the believer would have to say. I met Ignacio Martin-Baro, you know, and he would not have wanted to be considered extraordinary. He knew the danger he was in, but he presented his work and lifestyle as simply the sort of response that any person of faith would feel bound to make in horrid conditions such as those of San Salvador."

*Deborah:* "Horrid conditions make ordinary virtue heroic —is that what you're saying?"

*John:* "Yes—at least, they can make ordinary virtue heroic. Telling the truth is the same, whether one is facing a friend or a deadly enemy. Yet, of course it's also completely different, because of the completely different consequences it can have. I run little risk in calling the Bush government despicable for supplying arms to right-wing military personnel who murder people calling for economic and political justice. If I were to do that in San Salvador, or to make a similar statement about the ruling regime in Iran, I might be courting assassination. The least suspicious martyrs are those who are slain because they simply tell the truth or act humanely in truthless, inhuman circumstances."

*Deborah:* "This conversation is giving me the willies. Fortunately, I don't have to put much on the line each day. Most of my moral dilemmas barely amount to a hill of beans. I don't want to think about what it would be like to play for such high stakes as those in El Salvador. May we scale this discussion back, so that it deals more with ordinary virtue in ordinary, relatively sane settings?"

*John:* "Gladly. I'm no more comfortable contemplating martyrdom than you are. I don't know what I would do, in circumstances where telling the truth became heroic, and I feel that I'm dramatizing when I try to imagine such a situation. Still, maybe there's a benefit in thinking about the unthinkable now and then. Maybe those who want all theology and ethics to be reviewed, in light of the *Shoah* or other catastrophes, have a point. I read an article the other day by a man amazed at his reaction to being diagnosed as having cancer. He has found it more exhilarating than depressing, because it has forced him to become serious and concentrate on what is really important to him."

*Deborah:* "I don't know about that. If events force us to reconsider our lives, fine. But is it healthy to make crisis into a norm or give it a privileged status? I know, you've already accused me of being addicted to crisis, but what we're talking about here is quite different. The destruction of six million Jews is something I can't get my mind around, and I'm sure there are other enormities in history that are similarly incomprehensible. I have thought about cancer, of course, and it shows up in my family's medical history. But I've decided that it's not healthy to brood about my chances of getting cancer, or about what changes I would have to make if I were to get cancer. The most

I've decided because of thinking about cancer is that I ought to try to get the maximum out of each day and not plan on a long, healthy old age."

*John:* "Still more complicated matters. On the one hand, crises occur, and the possibility of crisis is a legitimate pressure to reflect about what is really important in life. On the other hand, it is morbid and unhealthy to make crisis the norm. So, I tend to agree that when a crisis does occur, we should take it as an occasion to remind ourselves of the fragility of life and re-commit ourselves to making the most of the present. Further, I tend to think that the gratitude I mentioned the other day should surface from the appreciation of the mysteriousness of human existence that crises underscore. In other words, evil and death should not be spotlighted, but they should be reckoned with. Ideally, when we reckon with them we reappreciate how health is the norm and sickness the deviance, and how virtue is the norm and sin the deviance. The butchery in El Salvador stands out because we have accepted decency, civility, and a common respect for human life as obvious, ordinary, bedrock assumptions. Cancer stands out because we have accepted good health as the rule, what is expectable. Now we're asking how to make the normal, the expectable, more precious in light of the threats to it. I think that's a *wonderful* question, in both senses of the word."

ৡৡ

*Deborah:* "Let me get back to my sense that ethics interests me more than religion. 'Religion' brings to my mind ceremonies in church, dogmatic teachings, and pious acts like reading the Bible or kneeling in prayer. Ethics brings to my mind pictures of people actually helping the poor, feeding the hungry, curing the sick. I find ethics much more compelling. Why should I care about the liturgical ceremonies or the dogmas that some people claim are the foundation for their ethical activism and idealism?"

*John:* "Perhaps you shouldn't care about such things, if ethics seems to you self-sufficient. Do you think that helping the poor, and feeding the hungry, and curing the sick can stand on their own, as self-evidently good, compelling activities?"

*Deborah:* "I start to say yes, but then I realize the obvious rejoinder: why, then, doesn't everyone rush to do such things? Indeed, why is my commitment to such things only part-time and occasional? When I started in the medical profession, I assumed that I would be doing good night and day. Now I work in an office, supervising a staff of nurses, and even though I tell myself that I'm making possible a wealth of health care, I worry that I've lost touch with my original idealism. There's something immediately rewarding about dealing with patients on a ward. To become an administrator requires quite an act of faith—sometimes a bigger one than I'm capable of. Still, I admire nurses, and doctors, and teachers, and social workers, because they are trying to make a difference. Compared to people who are simply out to make money, those in the helping professions seem to me more significant. I suspect that you would like me to reflect on the implications of such a value judgment. That's your regular line, you know: reflect on the implications. It's difficult."

*John:* "The examined life is very difficult, and I certainly flee from it as regularly as I encourage it. Knowledge makes a bloody entrance, and knowledge of this sort throws us back into the mysteriousness of our human venture."

*Deborah:* "Is that what the church ceremonies and dogmas are supposed to handle, the mysteriousness of the human venture? Are you saying that they can stabilize ethical idealism, by giving people some purchase on a God who makes it good to dedicate oneself to social service rather than making money? I'm leery of that. Most of the church ceremonies I've attended have been boring, and dogma is the last thing I need. I would have thought that laying down the law, telling people what they have to believe, would repulse you, too, since you're always going on about integrity and spiritual freedom."

*John:* "Getting a little riled up, aren't we? And somewhat unnecessarily. 'Dogma' has come to mean a heavy-handed, authoritarian approach to doctrine, but originally it simply meant truths of faith that had been certified by authoritative Christian leaders. In contrast to speculation or opinion, dogma was something you could rely upon, something the entire Christian community held as truth important to salvation. Since the Enlightenment, we moderns have had a hard time with dogma, because it challenges our claims to autonomy. Undeniably, Christian church leaders have often abused the notion of dogma, imposing ideas or practices that should have been left optional. But in itself dogma is simply a logical extension of revelation—the fact that divinity has made itself known in ways that human beings on their own could not have imagined. And revelation is a logical, if breathtaking, response of God to the human predicament: if human beings cannot fathom their situation, if they need guidance to avoid disaster, then it makes sense for a good creator to supply them with such guidance. Ultimately, of course, the 'guidance' that the creator supplies is not so much information as the divine love itself. Ultimately, the core of revelation is God's self-disclosure and self-offer, which for Christians is enfleshed in Jesus of Nazareth. And, finally, this self-offer is the justification for worship. Were it properly understood and properly enacted, Christian liturgy would be the most beautiful of celebrations, because it would be a loving communion with a God so good he put himself out to realign our warped situation."

*Deborah:* "More mystification. Are you saying that dogma

ought to give ethics a sure foundation, by rooting it in truths that God has revealed, and that worship ought to convince people that God is not only a law-giver but also someone wanting to communicate with them in love?"

*John:* "I am indeed. You've got a great knack for boiling my too many words down to the essence."

*Deborah:* "The problem still remains, though: a lot of religious teaching is dogmatic, in the pejorative sense, and a lot of religious ceremonial is boring. That seems to leave you in the position of basing your faith on an ideal rather than an actual practice. You're forced to tell me to disregard the actual practice and contemplate what ought to be—what could be, if religious people knew what they were doing or were fully mature in their faith. Is that ethical? Isn't disregarding actual practice and stressing the ideal an evasion of the praxis that those liberation theologians you mentioned make primary? Doesn't it violate common sense? If you told me to disregard the actual practice of a surgeon and concentrate on his ideals, I'd think you were his lawyer in a malpractice suit."

*John:* "What a tiger you are. We'd better get you back on the wards, so that you remember how difficult actual practice can be. Kidding aside, though, of course you're nearly completely right. If people find religion badly practiced, why should they pursue it? All I can say in response is that God is not contained by 'religion,' and that when one encounters God the reasons for worship ceremonies and religious doctrines become quite clear. At the same time, the failures of religious bodies become more depressing, because one has glimpsed what ought to be and realized that frequently those professing to be God's friends are the biggest obstacles to others' faith. Eventually, however, one also realizes that humankind cannot bear much reality, as T.S. Eliot said, and that one's own life is shot through

25

with weakness and hypocrisy. So, eventually, the scandals of the religious bodies become less scandalous, and one has to worry about crossing the line between accepting human weakness and condoning a shabby service of God. The only caveats I would place on your challenge, then, run to the conclusion that we don't have any other choice. Worship and doctrinal clarification are natural, good effects of religious experience. When one meets God, one wants to respond with proper praise, and one wants to understand correctly what has happened. But the problem of losing the original spirit among the letters of tradition is the tragic puzzle of religious existence."

*Deborah:* "If I understand you, then, it is valid to judge religious bodies by the quality of religious or simply human living they foster, yet we cannot equate the truth of their ideals with the shabbiness of their performance. That's either a subtle cop-out or a significant challenge to the working categories of a pragmatist like me. I tend to think that handsome is as handsome does. I'd even extend that to God: God is as God does. But I can see that God is a special case, not being susceptible to empirical examination like handsome Bill or Tom. Is God then non-verifiable or non-falsifiable? How can God lose, if one has to distinguish between the only things one can test, the people representing God, and God himself or herself? You're just making me more hungry for something I can nail down, like ethical activity."

*John:* "I'm sorry, but that's not really my fault. God is by definition different, unique. One finally has to make an act of faith, for or against the reality or goodness of the basal mystery I've been referring to. Ethical activity is a fine indicator of such faith, but no finite indicator can specify fully the infinite divinity, and no ethical activity that we can examine is without ambiguity. So we're stuck with mysteriousness on all sides, and the best we can do is keep it from becoming mystification."

ᢅᠥ

*Deborah:* "So, once again we're back to the proposition that ethics, like everything else, takes us into the mysteriousness that you want to call divine. That mysteriousness alone doesn't need an explanation, is primordial and self-explanatory. But what does that mysteriousness explain? Maybe it's just a quirk of our minds: we can imagine to the point where we defeat our own imagination and so start to speak negatively—"infinite," "beyond rational grasp," "without dependence or regress." Aren't those the kinds of words philosophers use? Those are the ones I remember from my course in the philosophy of religion."

*John:* "Those are the words, but theologians and people of faith are not limited to them. If one takes one's stand on the story of Jesus, letting it guide one's reflections about the foundations of human existence, then the mysteriousness turns out to be the nearness of the divine being, which grants all of us both our being and our destiny. Christian philosophy says that we only exist because God has granted us a share in the being that God alone possesses independently. Christian theology says that our reason for being, our destiny, is to be loved by God and love God back, in return. The Israelite prophets use the figure of marriage. Human destiny is to be wedded to the force, the personal love, that has brought all things into being. At death and the climax of history, the marriage will be consummated, so that our being with God, who is infinite love, will perdure endlessly and be endlessly fulfilling. All of this carries a certain logic, but it is not the logic of the philosophers of religion. It is the logic of a divine lover who boggles our minds and seduces our hearts by his goodness. God is not too strange to be believed but too good."

*Deborah:* "That sounds like a contemplative theologian

who has thought himself off the map. Jesus I can understand. He said that the love of his Father ought to show itself in the sorts of deeds he himself performed: curing the sick, casting out demons, teaching those longing to know about justice and God. He said that if people wanted, they could make a society just and caring. Isn't that what the 'reign of God' implied: a society worthy of God, so fully human that it reflected God? This talk about everlasting life in love with God stretches far beyond the message I find in the gospels."

*John:* "How long since you've read the gospel of John?"

*Deborah:* "Quite some time, as it's quite some time since I've frequented a church or tried to pray. But I haven't forgotten the wonderful gospel scenes where Jesus cures the sick and frees the demoniacs. They played a part in my decision to go into nursing. As I said, my parents were not religious. I had a pious aunt, though, and she used to read Bible stories to me. Then, in college, I took a lot of courses in the humanities, because I liked them. They dealt with the big questions that interested me: questions of values, key choices, what a person ought to do with her life, what to make of suffering and love and chance. The gospels were a great relief, because they were concrete and vivid. I didn't understand all of the cultural implications—the background of the parables, for instance—but I had a good teacher, and he brought the teachings of Jesus to life."

*John:* "Well, to cut to the chase: the gospel of John, though more theological and mystical than the synoptics, presents an interpretation of the actual life of Jesus that the early Christian community found compelling. In that interpretation, Jesus is a great many things, but divine Wisdom (the very Word of God enfleshed) is at the center. The Johannine Jesus makes faith the gateway to love, light, and life. Indeed, these three conse-quences of joining with God, the Father of Jesus, through faith cohere. The life that one joins is a fullness of light and love. The love is what God is, the force that accounts for creation and is stronger than death. The light is truth created by the divine love. To abide with the Father, with Christ, with their Spirit is to become divinized—a partaker of the divine nature, which is love, life, and light. So, the Johannine interpretation of the Jesus who cures, instructs, works powerful signs of God's power in him, and suffers and dies in fidelity to his mission is that this Jesus is fully divine—so fully divine that union with him in faith divinizes his followers. From that thesis, it follows that the mysteriousness we find on all sides of human consciousness should be interpreted as a personal creative love soliciting our response and holding out the prospect of everlasting fulfillment."

*Deborah:* "So now we've got the entire agenda unveiled. You maintain the quite traditional view that there is a heaven, a place of complete fulfillment. You say that the desires we feel can find a response, a consummation. You locate the way to this consummation in Christian faith, and you interpret Jesus as not merely a splendid human being, powerfully able to alleviate people's miseries, but also literally divine, a presence of the holy force that made the world and might heal our broken humanity. How can you carry all this baggage? Why isn't Jesus the ethical teacher, the great healer, the archetypal representative of innocent humanity done to death by human evil enough?"

*John:* "I love the full humanity of Jesus, the splendid language and power and compassion that flow out of him, as the different New Testament authors portray him. And I am mesmerized by his suffering, which, as you say, is the archetypal representation of innocent humanity brought face to face with the human will to hurt and destroy truths it cannot abide. To my mind, there is nothing comparable in human history: not the wisdom of the Buddha, nor the death of Socrates, nor the binding of Isaac. But, there is more than this full humanity in all the gospels, synoptic as well as Johannine, to say nothing of the Pauline literature, the book of Revelation, the epistle to the Hebrews, and even the pastoral letters. For Mark, Jesus is the mysterious conqueror of Satan, the powerful innocent whose need to suffer confounds his disciples and makes Christian existence counter-cultural to the core. For Matthew, Jesus is the fulfillment of messianic prophecy, including the Isaiahan prophecies about the suffering servant. For Luke, Jesus is not only the fulfillment of Jewish messianic expectation but also the light and salvation for which the Gentiles have yearned. For John, Jesus is the Word of God enfleshed, come to reveal the love in God's heart and invite people to share divine life. All of these evangelical theologies, without exception, are structured by faith that the resurrection of Jesus cast an entirely new light on his career and person. What had seemed a noble failure by worldly standards, a victory only in the spiritual order, became a complete success, when the Father raised Jesus from death and established him at the divine 'right hand.' One needed new categories to describe the reality of Jesus and the significance of his life and death. Very quickly, the early Christians filled the categories available to them from the surrounding culture, Jewish and Hellenistic alike, with new meaning. To say that Jesus was a prophet, or the messiah, or the Son of God, or a holy man, or a rabbi, or even a priest was to change those categories as much as find them serviceable. The end of the long process of trying to make sense of Jesus that the gospels began is not in sight, but the guidelines that have become regulative for the Christian mainstream are clear. Jesus should be considered both fully human and fully divine. To deny either his full humanity or his full divinity is to speak heretically—in opposition to mainstream, authoritative Christian tradition. No proper sophistication about either the history of Christian faith or the philosophy of Christian language takes away the necessity or centrality or full force of this dual affirmation. For Christian thinkers who know their business and want to follow the great cloud of witnesses who have preceded them in handing on the faith, the conjoined humanity and divinity of Christ have to be the origin and touchstone of specifically Christian utterance and culture."

§∂

*Deborah:* "I have to respect your desire to be orthodox in your Christian faith. Clearly, speaking in concert with the mainstream of Christian faith is important to you. But you must know that such speech is an anachronism, even though you vary the traditional formulas with new images and take them somewhat symbolically. In my experience, the vast majority of Americans divide into two camps. Either they are secularized people for whom traditional Christian language is at best a bit of nostalgia, and at worst an impediment to realistic dealing with today's world. Or, they are fundamentalist Christians who take the Bible literally and so seem stupid or caught in a time warp. The number of Americans striving earnestly to create a faith intellectually respectable, a faith that could stir contemporary minds the way Gregorian chant or the music of Palestrina used to stir Christian emotions, is pitifully small. There isn't one doctor in twenty at our hospital who would understand what you're talking about."

*John:* "But you understand what I'm talking about?"

*Deborah:* "Somewhat. I know you. We've been talking about serious matters for several years. And once upon a time I did read the Bible seriously and I did study world religions, Christianity included. Even for me, though, your freshening of traditional images to interpret Jesus is a stretch. You want to stay close to his humanity, as the gospels portray it, and yet you also want to invest that humanity with the power, the being, of divinity. How can you have it both ways?"

*John:* "I can have it both ways if I'm following mainstream Christian understanding of the New Testament presentation of

Jesus. And I can have it both ways if it turns out that humanity and divinity are coordinated to one another—that humanity can express divinity, and divinity is what humanity strives to join itself with, for its fulfillment."

*Deborah:* "Let's take those two arguments one at a time. First, how much do you depend on the New Testament? What separates you from the fundamentalist?"

*John:* "I depend on the New Testament a great deal, because it has been *the* text at the foundations of Christian faith. Whether one speaks of the articulate, sophisticated faith of the great Christian theologians, or the lay faith of the vast hordes of ordinary Christian believers, the New Testament has provided the matrix, the fundamental range of images and convictions on which all else has depended. I differ from the fundamentalist, though, because I want to work out my understanding of Christ, and of human existence, from a New Testament that only comes fully alive when it is heard in the context of worship, and when its resonances mingle with the interpretations of the saints and bright teachers who have pondered it through the ages. The fundamentalist rips the New Testament from its natural context, which is the community from which it arose and for which it was written—a community most fully itself at the eucharistic liturgy and most articulate in its holiest and most learned members. I want to develop my understanding of faith and reality as a member of the Christian community, even though there are many things about the politics and past history of that community that I abhor."

*Deborah:* "What about the second argument, concerning the correlation of humanity and divinity?"

*John:* "Well, that can be taken simply or technically. Simply, I find that human beings are the richest metaphors of God, the most intriguing expressions. Here the code-word tying my intuition to the tradition is the biblical notion, much developed by the church fathers, that human beings are 'images' of God.

From the other side, I also find that divinity is what the human being seeks for its fulfillment. Only an infinite fullness of light and love, truth and goodness, would satisfy the drives at the core of the human make-up, the drives to know and love without restriction. Here the tie to the tradition could be Augustine's phrase, 'You have made us for yourself, O God, and our hearts are restless until they rest in you.' "

*Deborah:* "Relate all this to my passion for ethics. Show me how the New Testament view of Jesus, or the traditional Christian coordination of divinity and humanity, enriches that passion. If you can do that, I might take you seriously."

*John:* "You mean you haven't been taking me seriously thus far? My, what a good actress you are."

*Deborah:* "Get on with it."

*John:* "O.K., I'll make a stab. Go to the depths of an exemplary ethical and religious hero such as Jesus, or the Buddha, or Mahatma Gandhi, and what do you find? You find a rationale for the admirable moral behavior. And this rationale is not just verbal. It is also passionate, a feature of the love and concern driving the hero to the acts, the dedication, the service of others that we admire so much. Jesus let his entire being repose in trust and love of his Father. He cured and preached and exorcised and suffered and died and rose because that was what following his Father's will, living out the mission that his trust and love of the Father created, led him to and required. The Buddha spent forty years teaching his *Dharma* because the light that flooded him required it. Out of compassion for the people suffering because they lived in ignorance, full of desires that enchained them, the Buddha had no choice but to offer others the fruits of his own liberating experience. Mahatma Gandhi found his vocation in South Africa, where what had been a lackluster career as an attorney blossomed into a series of experiments with the political potential of truth. Gandhi knew that the treatment of colored in South Africa was untrue—a lie, offending the dignity that all human beings possess. As he followed this intuition, he came to think that Truth is the universal name of God, and that if one relies on the truth it will prove liberating, politically as well as religiously. Thus Gandhi called his rationale *satyagraha*, the force that the truth carries, and that rationale informed all his fasts and strikes and marches. If we use these three exemplary ethical people, the religious roots of truly liberating, transformative ethical actions become clear. One finally does the right thing, especially the right thing that requires sacrifice, because one has a conception of reality amounting to a reverence for, even a service of, what is Right and Good—a conception in which something is capitalized, called holy and wonderfully imperative. Now, the view of Jesus that I've just crammed into a few sentences is laid out at some length in the New Testament. You can't read Jesus as simply a good, ethical man without mutilating the primary sources on which all responsible interpretations of Jesus have to depend. If you ask how I justify the coordination of humanity and divinity that I've proposed, I finally must point to the coincidence of the two in Jesus. There you find what can happen to a human being when he or she identifies with divinity completely, and there you also find what divinity is most like in human terms. But if Jesus is 'like us in all things save sin,' as traditional Christian faith claims, then the fulfillment that Jesus found in his Father, and the manifestation of the Father that Jesus' contemporaries found in his person and work, can apply analogously to any of us other human beings. Our sin makes a considerable difference, but it does not obliterate the solidarity between us and Jesus in possessing humanity—being creatures of flesh and spirit invited and forced to grapple with a pervasive mysteriousness. In a word, then, the New Testament portrait of Jesus, and such theological consequences of it as the coordination of humanity and divinity that I have sketched, provide the ground and third dimension of any ethical activity that I consider significant. Doing good, whether heroically or prosaically, is so much richer when interpreted in Christian symbolism that I find a Christian humanism far preferable to a secular interpretation."

# 3

# The Problem
# of the Churches

*Deborah:* "I'll think about your claim that religious faith gives a third dimension to ethical activity. And I like the way you speak of metaphor, because it suggests that we are all involved in a grand poetry—the evolving universe as an epic work. But you've been slighting the role of the churches in Christian faith. What does one do when the typical house of worship one visits is not appealing? How does one sift through the verbiage that fills the airwaves and often devalues the gospel? I don't need to remind you that feminists have axes to grind when it comes to the churches. For every woman who applauds the churches that stand against abortion there is at least another who charges the churches with a callous disregard of women's right to control their own bodies. Certainly, there are admirable people in the churches. But there is also fraud and stupidity and self-service. Don't you have to evaluate the enrichment that religion can bring to ethics in the context of the obstacles that the churches create for faith?"

*John:* "I think anyone has to deal with the actual performance of a given church fully honestly, with no axe to grind. There are good reasons for thinking that the church, the entire body of Christian believers, is an essential part of what theologians call the economy of salvation, but that shouldn't shield any particular congregation from frank criticism."

*Deborah:* "Well, then, let's take a few groups and discuss their impact. I suppose the sorriest ones are the followers of disgraced leaders like Jim Bakker. They look like fools, or masochists eager to be bilked. Don't they, both followers and leader, suggest that belonging to a Christian community can warp one's common sense, and even one's integrity?"

*John:* "They do indeed. Perhaps you know the old Latin saying, 'Corruptio optimi pessimum.' The corruption of the best thing makes the worst thing. The Bakkers of the religious world seem to get caught up in the emotional side of religion, eventually substituting the highs of performing and being applauded for the substance of religious service, which ought to be a sober confession that one is only doing what God seems to require. Indeed, the best ministers of God count themselves unprofitable servants and realize how seldom they give God full interest on the investment God has made in them."

*Deborah:* "What are we to conclude from that? Are you saying that religion is dangerous psychologically? That it can tip over psyches not well rooted in humility or realism or self-confidence? Wouldn't that play into charges like Nietzsche's that Christianity is a religion for the weak, and that it has crippled humanity's drive to maturity?"

*John:* "That's a whole string of questions. First, I would say that professing religious convictions publicly and taking a leadership role is dangerous psychologically—but so is entering politics, or working as a physician, or lecturing as a college professor. Any profession that exalts its practitioners carries psychological risks. Ironically, the best protection against them is a combination of quite ordinary gifts, such as a good sense of humor, and rare virtue, such as appreciating profoundly the implications of one's creaturehood—or at least of one's mortality. Second, I think there are, or certainly have been, ways in which religion in general and Christianity in particular have retarded people's maturity. On the other hand, I don't think that Nietzsche is the best model of emotional stability, and I think that Marx truncated both history and human nature unforgivably. For every hindrance that religion has thrown up, it has created a stimulus to create, grow, and serve the common good. As many people have noted, the roots of culture, both historical and psychological, are inseparable from cultus—profound reverence for the mysteries of human existence."

*Deborah:* "O.K., let's take another Christian group. Both the Catholics and the Eastern Orthodox have stressed cultus. Both have developed an elaborate liturgical tradition, though since Vatican II the Catholics may have given theirs short shrift. I can understand the aesthetic appeal of a Russian Orthodox liturgy or Catholic high mass—mainly because they can be sung to glorious music. A Mozart Kyrie can be thrilling. But many Christians who find such liturgical ceremonies appealing seem to want to live in the middle ages. They yearn for a time when the sacred and the secular were one, a time when culture was integral rather than pluralistic. I find that more nostalgic than realistic. The fact is that we live in a very secular, pluralistic culture. The large pockets of fundamentalism notwithstanding, academic and professional life in the United States has little truck with religion of the mystical kind that you have been proposing. If you work for a large hospital, as I do, or for IBM, or for the government, an enthusiasm for Gregorian chant or the sermon on the mount makes you eccentric. It's fine for you to water the garden of your spirit with Eastern Orthodox liturgical music, and IBM may pat you on the back for leading a Sunday school class, as well as wearing a button-down shirt and voting Republican, but any serious religiosity—any that challenges the corporation's commitment to the bottom line—will get you in deep trouble."

*John:* "Let's deal first with the charge of nostalgia. I think it's real, but not simple. On the one hand, we're not living in the middle ages, or in an Eastern Christian realm where church and state both come under the emperor. On the other hand, there is something healthy in wanting an integral culture, and the paeans to pluralism that one sometimes hears are misguided. The middle ages, and the eastern realms, had their considerable problems, and I'm quite sure that neither you nor I would like to be transported back to them. But they were saner than our contemporary western civilizations, because they had a clear sense of what a human life ought to accomplish. The vicious aspect of our pluralism is the way it dovetails with a practical atheism. Religious convictions having become nearly completely private, the transcendent realm evoked by the name 'God' has little force in our common, public life. As a result, we lack the perspective necessary for wisdom of any significant sort. We don't use our resources well. Our domestic and foreign policies easily devolve into power-politics and expediency. We live as though there were no judgment of God, no final arbitration worth taking into account. The wonder is that we don't have more influential nihilists. So, I agree that we have to live in the culture that actually obtains, but I won't criticize people who frequent rich Christian liturgies (or theologies) in search of ballast and balance for their souls."

*Deborah:* "But hasn't our pluralism rendered the harmonies assumed and sought by traditional liturgies impossible? Don't we have to accept the fact that the typical modern soul is fragmented, little prepared to love silence or pray contemplatively or shape public policies in terms of the common good? American individualism is so strong that people don't know the language of the common good, the priority of the whole over the part. If we did we wouldn't have the millions of homeless who disgrace our society. We wouldn't have the indigents who come into our clinics and, by their simple being, mock the huge mess we've made of medical insurance. The capitalistic system we've developed has no place for the poor, those who can't compete, even those who through no fault of their own are sick or need help. It runs by mammon, and you know what Jesus said about mammon."

*John:* "I do indeed. I just wish the alternatives to capitalism were clearer. In theory, socialism is much preferable. But in practice, we find few socialisms that work well economically or excite human creativity to the full. Maybe a few small collectives succeed and stimulate both work and art that is 'popular,' in the sense of and for the people as a whole. But even the Scandinavian countries, where one might say that socialism has worked fairly well, have significant problems—widespread alcoholism, for example. I wouldn't deny the proposition that American capitalism has created greater problems, but I'm leery of doctrinaire alternatives. Still, I think that the longing for community, and the desire to return political thought to the priority of the common good (including, most emphatically, the good of the ecosphere), is more healthy than unrealistic. The great problem is to motivate people to use their individual liberties idealistically, for the good of all rather than simply their own profit. And that, of course, is where one ought to fault the churches very seriously. They have not made persuasive the idealism, the self-sacrifice, the joy in living a spare, simple life dedicated to a significant spiritual cause, that their claims to represent God require. With a few wonderful exceptions, they have supported the dysfunctional status quo more than they have challenged it prophetically or shown how it might be reoriented by a return to the perennial philosophy, the love of wisdom that made God the alpha and omega of all sane calculations."

ᵹᴇ

*Deborah:* "That's fine rhetoric, but what is it going to mean to the typical employee of IBM or Mobil or General Electric or AT&T? They crunch numbers all day, or pore over computers, or try to figure out how to get the world to buy more of their products. The perennial philosophy has about as much hold on their spirits as Taoist poetry. God is not a player in their world. Transcendence, divinity, Jesus, the Buddha—none of the many facets of the religious world makes an impact. We have a generation of people—maybe several generations—who work 'as if God were not given,' to quote a line from Bonhoeffer that has never left me. Granted, some of them do drugs, because they cannot stand living in flatland, and others are miserably unhappy they know not why. Granted, their personal relationships tend to flounder, and a good marriage, with contented spouse and kids, is hard to find. But they represent mainstream American professionalism. The message the churches give out barely dents their hides. That's why they stay away in droves. That's why mainstream American denominations are shrinking and growth is confined to the evangelical fringes."

*John:* "Well, you've made a lot of generalizations, and I'm not sure that the best sociologists of contemporary American religion would agree with you. But I have a lot of sympathy for the mood in which you speak. Popular American culture does seem to have little soul. Drugs and awful music and a careening search for 'fun' do call to mind the foyers of hell. The poor shrivel into depression, because their condition seems hopeless. Many of the affluent lead lives no sane person could consider significant. A friend of mine teaching at an eastern college told me that the seniors at his school wanted Donald Trump for their commencement speaker. The height of their ambition was

41

the art of the deal. So, often it does seem that people are ignorant unto the death of their own souls. But, a closer scrutiny
again makes things more mysterious. One of the many paradoxes of the human condition is that people can know they are
doing themselves in, can hate the boredom and triviality and
selfishness that dominate them night and day. This is not simply
a preacher's pious hope. It is something confirmed every day in
thousands of counselors' offices, to say nothing of tens of thousands of neighborhood bars. For a person of faith, there is no
escape from the question of God. Not even cultural amnesia,
rampant practical atheism, can change the fact that we have
been made for God. We choke unless we are breathing the clean
air of significant purpose. Our reach always exceeds our grasp.
The task of people like me who write, and people in the
churches who minister more practically, is to believe in this
human thirst for meaning and find ways to correlate it with a
credible gospel."

*Deborah:* "Let me ask you about a third group of churches,
whose gospel is incredible to me, somewhat to my own surprise.
I mean those groups that consider a woman's right to abortion
more important than the preservation of innocent life in the
womb. I am a nurse. I know very well the horrors of the old
days, when abortion was a back-alley industry. The last thing I
want is to return to those days. But I'm sickened by the political
turn that the controversy about abortion has taken, and I'm
amazed that women who have actually given birth and are raising children should block out the implications of carrying new
human life. Of course, there are all sorts of grounds for legitimate differences of opinion about when we should call uterine
life human. What I can't get my mind around, though, is the
spectacle of religious people exalting freedom of choice so fer-
vently that they collude with an obscene carelessness about life
in the womb. If anything is sacred, it is the newborn child,

miraculous in its tiny perfection and innocence. To thwart the process that creates that miracle, after any significant progress toward it (certainly after the first trimester), is one of the few truly heinous acts I can imagine."

*John:* "Strong words, but I think I understand. Abortion is such a mess. I know one doctor who used to perform abortions but stopped immediately after a young girl he had helped told him he was the nicest abortionist she could imagine and she'd recommend him to all her friends. She had no idea how she'd insulted him, or made him come to himself and reconsider what being a physician meant. On the other hand, we both know that many pregnancies are disasters, by any human reckoning. It's not hard to understand why people can think that, for the good of the woman involved, and in view of the dismal future they foresee for the child, abortion provides a neat solution. I don't know how to adjudicate all of that. I'm grateful week after week that I'm not an ethicist, forced to do so. My whole instinct is that we've got to stop using abortion as a contraceptive. That cheapens life so drastically that it ought, logically, to open the door to any enormity. Why not infanticide, if the newborn proves unacceptable? Why not eugenics and euthanasia and all the other extensions of human power into the administration of life and death? On the other hand, again, we're dealing with millions of people who feel so put upon, or are so abandoned by society at large, that the prospect of caring for undesired human lives seems intolerable. Abortion is a function of the entire way we've constructed our common culture. We can't separate it from the plight of the elderly, or the handicapped, or the homeless, or the mentally ill. It's ironic, to say the least, that some of the churchpeople most adamant about abortion rights are leading the charge for those other needy groups. It's equally ironic, I suppose, that some of the churchpeople most eloquent about the evils (cultural, as well as moral) of abortion are associated with caveats about contraception and sex education, the most obvious remedies. Really, it makes my head swim, and sometimes I hide behind the fact that I'm a male to beg off from dealing with it."

*Deborah:* "Well, for our purposes abortion is only an illustration, so I won't press you any further. As I said, I've been surprised at my own reaction to zealous advocates of abortion rights, especially those claiming membership in Christian churches. If Christianity can be interpreted so differently by various Christians, what happens to its credibility?"

*John:* "You tell me. What impact has the division among Christians about American policy on nuclear arms, or about principles of economic justice, made on you?"

*Deborah:* "You mean controversies about the Catholic bishops' pastoral letters and similar church statements? I guess that has intrigued me, but not scandalized me the way that the division about abortion rights has. Maybe it's just that I feel I know the technical side of the abortion issue quite well, but that I'm a hopeless amateur when it comes to nuclear weapons, or military strategy, or economic policy. My instincts are very liberal. I feel that nuclear weapons are an abomination, and that the way our society distributes wealth is indefensible. Every time I read about the cost of a stealth bomber, and then consider the tide of homeless people in our society, I feel that I'm living in an asylum. Part of what I'm longing for is clear guidelines, issued by a disinterested, wise group such as the Christian church might be. And I guess many Christian thinkers have done a lot of work on such matters as disarmament, non-violence, alternatives to our present rape of nature, and the like. But they haven't created a clear, obvious alternative to our current cultural drift. Or we haven't let ourselves hear them. There's always the problem of people being unwilling to hear the gospel, I suppose."

ॐ

*John:* "You suppose correctly. Sometimes the churches preach the gospel quite well but society at large turns a deaf ear. We no longer live in a Christian culture. One can't assume that an appeal to the manifest intent of scripture or Christian tradition will be suasive. Churches have to be careful not to make this apparent fact into a defense for their own failures, but they also have to factor it into their self-criticisms. Jesus himself had many walk away, unwilling to take his message to heart. No doubt after several such occasions, he quoted the prophet Isaiah on the mystery of God's dulling people's hearts, so they might hear but not understand. People have to want to be converted, if the gospel is to make its full impact on them. They have to be hungering and thirsting for a deeper life. One of the worst results of our current popular culture is the way it numbs so many people against feeling either the pain or the joy that might make them passionate for a deeper life."

*Deborah:* "Is that why some Christian thinkers stress the conflict between the gospel and spontaneous human desire or aspiration? I've never quite understood the debate between those who say that Christianity is a religion, fulfilling the natural aspirations of human beings, and those who deny that it is a religion, because they take it to be something coming from a holy God who devastates all human pride and creation. To my mind, a Christianity so antagonistic to human aspiration would have a terrible problem making itself appealing. The advantage I see in your stress on the mysteriousness of the human condition is that it gives Christian theology common ground with all people's experience. But I suppose that has its problems, because otherwise there wouldn't be heavyweight theologians criticizing it."

*John:* "Yes, there are problems with both positions. If the churches take a hard line, perhaps basing themselves on the saying of Paul that he wanted to preach only Christ crucified, they risk speaking only to the converted, or to the converted and those so desperate that they find Kierkegaard's leap of faith or Tertullian's notion of believing because of absurdity attractive. They abandon responsibility for culture at large, set themselves up to become a beleaguered minority, if not a sect of puritans, and default on the rich humanism implicit in the incarnation. On the other hand, if they forget the cross of Christ, and the lesson Paul learned when preaching to the learned in Athens (they dismissed him as just another philosopher with just another interesting opinion), the churches risk being coopted by the times they live in. Karl Barth, one of the most eloquent exponents of the view that the gospel and culture are in an antagonistic relationship, made a powerful case for the awesome transcendence of God, and so the utter priority of God's initiatives. Barth is associated with the heroic German Confessing Church that stood up to Hitler, and that association shows the strength of the antagonistic position, when it comes to the need to oppose truly diabolical cultural movements such as Nazism. In the Catholic camp, Hans Urs von Balthasar, a favorite of Pope John Paul II, was similarly insistent that the church has to keep faith with its own divinely given mission and structure. Balthasar did not accept the metaphysics implied in Barth's position, because of his schooling in the Catholic tradition of analogy, and also because of his love for the Johannine christology, which makes divine revelation thoroughly enfleshed. But Balthasar did criticize those, such as Karl Rahner, who tried to make common human experience the basic locus of divine presence and used such experience not only to work out a contemporary spirituality but also to criticize the churches, when they seemed out of touch with the experience of ordinary lay people. My own sympathies are divided, since I see much truth in the instincts of Barth and Balthasar, but on the whole Rahner is more congenial to me, because I love the idea that God is everywhere, drawing all people through the common human project of trying to create a meaningful existence and become a person of honesty and love."

*Deborah:* "If you use a secular person such as me as your touchstone, it's Rahner by a landslide. I want the churches to speak from a solidarity with me in my ordinary human experiences, trials, hopes, and needs. I don't want sermons from the mountain top, even though I am moved by the sermon on the mount. It is the man Jesus, moving among his fellow human beings, curing and teaching and loving, who makes Christianity credible to me. That's also why I am staggered by the churches, such as the Roman Catholic and the Eastern Orthodox and the fundamentalist Protestant, that have a hard time treating women as the equals of men. If they took their stand on obvious human experience, and tried to make the gospel illumine what each half of the human race has learned and needs, they would see in a flash that women have as many rights to the gospel, as many rights grounded in the gospel, as men. Indeed, when I read the gospels I see Jesus as concerned about helping women as about helping men, and I write off any patriarchalism in the text because it seems so obviously a given of the cultural situation in which Jesus worked, like the position of the torah or the political power of Rome."

*John:* "Rahner doesn't stand alone, of course. Lonergan and Schillebeeckx, who have been at least as influential as Balthasar, are also more sympathetic to ordinary human experience, individual and political alike, than those who find the gospel and culture antagonistic. The irony, moreover, is that all five of the theologians we've mentioned—Barth, Balthasar, Rahner, Lonergan, Schillebeeckx—received an excellent education in the Christian tradition and self-consciously strove to be faithful to that tradition, even as they tried to update it or communicate it to a new generation. One has to be ignorant or ill-willed to accuse any of them of denaturing the gospel. Even when they criticized one another, they assumed a common commitment to the faith long handed down and were mainly pointing out dangers they saw, should certain emphases become exaggerated."

*Deborah:* "I think the emphases that have become exaggerated are, on the one hand, the capitulation to the status quo that one finds in many wealthy churches, where the people seem to equate church-going and patriotism rather mindlessly, and, on the other hand, the exaggerated prophecy that one finds in a few fringe churches or church groups, where pacifism is obligatory and virtually all structures, ecclesiastical or governmental, are considered anathema. In the mainstream, where there is a tension between being in the world but not being of it, the majority of churches about which I find anything to admire attempt a balancing act. Usually they err on the side of accommodation or prudence, not preaching a gospel that I would call radical in a good sense, but one has to admire their efforts to challenge people without losing sight of what such people have to put up with in order to survive in our culture. For people with families, who need jobs and friends outside the church circle, some accommodation, if not compromise, is a strict necessity. At my hospital one has to accept the fact that physicians are interested in handsome salaries, as well as in alleviating pain and prolonging life. One also has to accept the fact that people want abortions, and often won't change their self-destructive lifestyles. You wouldn't believe the incidence of alcoholism, drug abuse, battered wives, incest, and other horrors that pass through our clinics in an average month. All of that impinges on what people find possible, as do the financial constraints that cutbacks in the oil industry and ripple effects from business takeovers create. Unless a church is willing and able to get involved with the real problems that people face, including the emotional upsets that afflict so many families, it is going to be written off as not knowing what it's talking about. I hold no brief for the involvement of groups such as Planned Parenthood in the movement to make abortion an unquestioned right, but I admire the work of such groups with unwed mothers and others who otherwise would not get prenatal care, as I admire their work in sex education and birth control. Real life is very messy. Those antagonistic to actual culture may be fleeing real life rather than preaching a pure gospel."

§☙

*John:* "What is your position on the increase of what many have called a 'therapeutic' stance in the helping professions, including church ministries? I take it the term means a stress on the problems or sicknesses that people face, leading to descriptions of ministers and other helpful types as 'wounded healers' and the like. The point often seems to be the emotional impact that traumas, great and small, create and so the need for counseling, support groups, and other ways of letting off steam and getting some perspective, or at least some sense of not being alone in one's depression or sense of upset."

*Deborah:* "I think such groups are more useful than not, though I agree that in some cases they may lead people to expect emotional problems and so help to create them. Some counseling is very useful, but other counseling seems to blink the fact that people have always had to deal with pain and loss, ultimately by relying upon a philosophy or faith that made some sense of them. The breakdown in traditional faith has created a market for psychological approaches to suffering. People have to have some system for coping. I just wonder whether psychology can deliver the deep meaning that serious suffering requires us to search out. On the other hand, much of the traditional pastoral theology was rationalistic, unable to mediate help that would touch people's emotions as well as their minds. The movement toward a more therapeutic approach may well reflect the impact of women's liberation, in that women have started to articulate a more holistic view of the human personality that lays considerable stress on feelings and connections to other people. That I also find more helpful than harmful, though it's not without its dangers."

*John:* "I guess my main doubt is that anything can substitute for the mysteriousness of human fate or the significance of Christ's cross. Once those are in place as bedrock realities and helps, any therapies that counseling or support groups might offer would be fine. People do need the touch and interest of other people. It is terrible that so many people live in isolation and have no relief from their pains. But it's also terrible that we haven't helped more people to pray about their troubles, complain directly to God, and experience the relief that the deepest perspectives can provide. We are all only creatures of a day. Pain is part of the common human lot. When we can face these bottom-line realities, a certain peace becomes available. It doesn't take away the pain, but it can take away the guilt many people seem to feel, their sense of failure."

*Deborah:* "That is strange, isn't it? Not only do people have to suffer physical pains or emotional losses, they also have to cope with feelings of failure. Because they have gotten sick, or lost a job, or not become a great success according to the standards trumpeted to them night and day by the media, they think themselves worthless. I don't know whether our turn to the therapeutic has more relieved this syndrome or exacerbated it. Certainly many people are helped when they can cry out their feelings of failure, but often the counselors don't go to the roots of such feelings, which tie into the mysteriousness you've stressed so much. I'm not sure I could tell people feeling worthless that God loves them in all circumstances, but I sure as hell wish someone could. That kind of talk can seem so commonplace, though, so debased, that it just doesn't do the job. I can't imagine myself saying, 'God loves you.' "

*John:* "I guess now we're getting down to it. What happens to a culture when the language of faith has become debased? How bereft people must feel, when they have to doubt even the words that used to be unimpeachable! If it no longer is credible that God so loved the world God gave the only begotten Son for our salvation, or that God numbers every hair of our heads in love, then our people are in heavy darkness indeed. My reaction, which may not be very helpful, is that soon after one has made the proper response to the legitimate question of why God permits suffering, pointing out the complexity of the issues involved, it's advisable to say that we don't know, that none of us can say, that we all have to find a way to cope and entrust ourselves to it. I believe that the Christian understanding of a mysteriously good God, combined with the central Christian symbolism of the death and resurrection of Jesus, is a powerful way to cope. I believe that millions of people have survived psychically by entrusting themselves to it. But I find that life and faith are regularly far more mysterious than even the best of our theologians appreciate. We've learned wonderful things about the human body, the natural world, and even the human psyche. But we haven't learned as much as we should have about how to cope with the radical mysteriousness of our condition. We haven't made it congenial to confess that we don't know, we can't know, we have to keep making acts of faith and asking God to give us the light that is good for us. This is very hard to say to people who want and in some ways need answers. It is very hard to transform into a medicine to soothe the great ache in their hearts. But sometimes real suffering makes people ready to hear it. Sometimes pain does appear in somber beauty to be the presence of a God too real to be pretty or nice."

*Deborah:* "I find the sufferings of children hardest to take.

Adults often have lived a good life, or have had good opportunities. I myself could say, if faced with a serious illness, 'Well, I've had a chance to experience many wonderful things.' But when I hear of a little child seriously ill, or being brought up in terrible circumstances, or abducted by some crazy person for God knows what terrible purpose, I feel overwhelmed. That is real darkness of spirit, and I can't imagine how parents cast into it manage to cope."

*John:* "Nor can I. I can only shut my mouth and offer my prayers, hoping against hope."

*Deborah:* "It is amazing, really, that despite all our technological progress we're still forced to hope against hope. Certainly, we've reduced many of the physical threats that people had to deal with prior to our century. But we haven't reduced the human liability to disease and evil—the terrifying possibilities that can make one wake up screaming. They seem to remain as constants, even though we try to distract ourselves and a great many of us enjoy worldly pleasures. What do such constants say about our human makeup? Do we create gods simply because we must have protectors against the terror?"

*John:* "I'm sure that's part of the reason. Often I've felt myself fighting to affirm my belief, because the alternative seemed unthinkable. My mind might pitch over, toward insanity or black panic, and I might never right it again. But even that seems more a defense of believing (and so I guess of the mission of the churches) than a condemnation or cause for scorn. If the real situation is that we are always liable to some unspeakable atrocity, some disaster caused by a sport of nature or human malice, then the wise response may be to cast ourselves into the keeping of the mystery, the void or fullness in our depths."

# 4

# *Injustice*

*Deborah:* "I have a friend who is in the last stages of liver cancer. What can I say to her? If 'God loves you' sticks in my throat, what is left to me? I'm not asking you for an answer, of course, I'm just wondering out loud about the present state of my spiritual resources."

*John:* "Why can't you say, 'God loves you'? Why can't you say, 'I love you'? If I were in your position, I'd probably feel equally tongue-tied. But that seems to me more a function of my own dividedness, my own not knowing fully enough what I believe, than of the reality or fittingness of God's love. In repose, back in my quiet apartment, the love of God sometimes seems the only thing one could base a life upon. Why I can't say that, or why I fear it would be impertinent, makes me cynical about my own faith."

*Deborah:* "That's refreshing to hear! I thought theologians had it all fitted together. Seriously, though, I think we all suffer a lack of confidence about expressing our deepest convictions or hopes. Partly, it's the fact that we don't know, with anything like the clarity we'd like to have, what we believe. Partly, it's the fact that our ordinary social discourse is so tame, so carefully contrived to steer away from serious issues. Most days I don't worry about this a great deal. But dealing with my very sick friend has made it troubling. She's relatively young—just at the stage where she should be enjoying the freedom of seeing her kids settled and her husband enjoying success and seniority in his work. I don't know how much she looked forward to time for her own interests, but I feel cheated for her. And hers is a common scenario, played out every day in hundreds of hospitals across our land. Certainly, many people live to a ripe old age and enjoy the chance to satisfy most of their ambitions. But enough do not to make me wonder about the fickleness of life, and about its justice. I think that's one of the key things that makes me leery of religious language, institutions, and faith. There is so much injustice in the world that to claim that God is in charge would be to indict God for terrible malpractice."

*John:* "I wonder what we ought to think about the apparently wasted hopes that a premature death seems to involve. Are they really wasted, or does the premature death itself represent a new opportunity, and so a new hope? That's a strange way to reason, I suppose, but it's one I can't get rid of. Who knows what is good for us—what time is 'premature'? You remember Socrates on his way to dying. His question—was his fate worse or better than the fate of those who would continue to live—has stuck with me. In the gospels, there is a similar play with the words 'life' and 'death.' True life is something working in the spirit, something that opens people to divine possibilities. True death is also something working in the spirit, closing people to those divine possibilities. So Jesus says that we should not fear the people who can slay our bodies, but the people who can inflict spiritual death. I know that that saying, like so many others, can be abused, but I think it remains burningly relevant. We all die—how long will it take our media mavens to come to grips with this elementary fact? Shouldn't our mortality make us question all of the judgments we blithely make about 'success' and 'failure'? Isn't part of the reticence or embarrassment we feel in the presence of the dying a confession that they stand in a privileged position, knowing more about what is truly important than we can know until we enter upon our own last days? I have always been impressed by the silence of the dying about their condition or the lessons they are drawing from it. It is as though they know it would be a waste of breath to speak to those who have not yet had death invade their flesh."

*Deborah:* "Yes, I've noticed that too. Sometimes I've intuited a parallel to what I feel in discussions with my daughter: there is no way that she can understand how I'm looking at her situation. And I suppose she shouldn't understand me. That is part of the mystery of the life-cycle. I can't remember fully what it was like to be eighteen, and she can't have the foggiest notion of what it is like to be forty-five. All the more so, I can't understand what it is like to be terminally ill, though of course I can use my imagination to wonder and so not be completely obtuse when dealing with someone who is dying. Still, I feel uncomfortable, even though I've spent hundreds of hours in the rooms of very sick people, trying to cheer their spirits and ease their passing."

*John:* "But is our dying, even our premature dying, really an injustice? Or is it simply another part of a vast mystery that we can't understand on any level, moral as well as scientific or philosophical, and so are bound to find scandalous? How much of what we instinctively label unjust is really an affront to our finitude? And how legitimate is it for the creature to complain that he or she can't understand the creator? You know that writers have spilt tankers of ink on the holocaust of six million Jews by the Nazis. On the one hand, it's obvious that the holocaust was a great evil and so a great scandal to people trying to understand God. On the other hand, I find some of the judgments passed on the holocaust premature and presumptuous. It's not that I want to say that good has come out of consummate evil. I'm not sure that anyone can say that, or that even if someone could it would redeem the evil. But I am sure that the full significance of the holocaust, as of any other compound and significant historical occurrence, is lost in the counsels of God. We don't know what happened in the souls of the so many different people in the so many different cellblocks. We can't say whether their final judgment on their own fate was a tribute to God or a cry of hatred. Perhaps they themselves could not have said. Such things run so deep, are so holistic, that no human being can get out of himself or herself enough to pass judgment. All the more, no human being can pass judgment on the final state of soul of another human being. Our 'soul' ties us into the mystery, the spiritual challenge, of the entire tissue of relationships emanating from our place in space, time, culture, and, for believers, the providential workings of God. We all have to hope that our good deeds really were good and our bad deeds, including our acts of apparent despair, were really not so bad that God, knowing all, could not forgive them. 'Even when our hearts condemn us, God is greater than our hearts'—has there ever been a more consoling line? If our final destiny is to find God, or be found by God, and commune with God endlessly, God's is the only verdict that counts. What is just or unjust, mature or premature, remains for God to decide, and our judgments, however necessary (because we have to make meaning as best we can), are always penultimate."

*Deborah:* "I understand what you're saying, and part of me responds to it positively—the part that loves the mysteriousness we have been probing. The great advantage I see in this position is that it writes no one off. What has seemed failure to human beings might be success to God, and vice versa. The one thing necessary in human life would be to please God, no doubt by loving one's fellow human beings well, and if one accomplished that one necessary thing, everything would fall into place, as either contributory or irrelevant. However, another part of me worries about pushing judgment off upon God. What if there is no God, or what if 'God' is simply the name and woolly concept we plug in when the mysteriousness threatens to break through our dikes? It is well for us to remember that our judgments have limited value, but surrendering everything into God's hands can be a prescription for terrible carelessness."

*John:* "I don't think that it usually is. Moreover, I don't think that reflecting on the ultimacy of God's judgments takes us completely apart from our own minds and hearts, our own consciences, because 'God' is a feature of our own souls. I'm not saying that God is the creation of our own souls, or that God has no independence of our thoughts and feelings or our cultural creations. But I think we have to realize that when we try to imagine the judgments of God, or when we play with the possible disparity between our human judgments and a judgment that would be truly ultimate, we are exercising human faculties. Certainly, those faculties have been raised and attuned by the workings of God that we call grace. Certainly, the con-naturality—spontaneous understanding—that occurs when one lives with God, in the abiding that the Johannine literature stresses, is at work. But it remains true that the ability to think about a truly ultimate judgment, and so imagine some of the paradoxes that such a thought suggests, is part of our human endowment. It wells up from our deepest spirit, in testimony to the fact that everything cultural is the product, as well as the conditioner, of our human constitution. We have built into us a desire for a comprehensive truth and an ability to preview what such a comprehensive truth would be like. 'Heuristically,' as the philosophers say, we know something precious about the nature and functions of the genuine God. So our consignment of ultimate judgment or significance to 'God' need not be an abdication of our human responsibility or makeup. It can be one of the fullest exercises of our human responsibility and makeup, because it can flow from our courageous confrontation of our own limits—of the border where our finite spirits run into the infinite, the borderless reality of the God who created us."

*Deborah:* "I'm not sure I followed all of that. Let me try to give it back. You're saying that our human makeup finally meets up with the infinity of God. God 'measures' us, in the sense that God is the reality that fences us in, limits our outreach. And because of this definition by God that is built into our human makeup, we have some inkling of how the judgments of God may be different from the judgments of human beings. At least, we have an experiential basis for keeping ourselves from thinking that what we make of a given situation is the last word, the God's-eye view. So, when we deal with a dying person, or our own guilt, we have to honor the fact that we are the creatures, not the creator—the pots, not the potter. If we do this, without ceasing to judge and act as we have to for social life to continue, we can keep our balance in the midst of a mysterious situation such as the apparently premature dying of a close friend."

*John:* "Very good indeed. The only thing that you missed was the Johannine 'abiding,' which when fully articulated leads theologians to speak of human beings' sharing in the life of the trinitarian persons, so that human knowing and loving swim in the stream of the divine knowing and loving. But all of that depends on one's accepting the privileged place of scripture and on an ability to contemplate the movements in one's own spirit in light of what scripture suggests."

*Deborah:* "Let me just nail something down. You would agree that doctors, nurses, family members, friends and any others who might rightly be involved have the obligation to deal with a dying person as helpfully as they can. You're not saying that because the judgments of God surpass human judgments we don't have to intervene for the patient's welfare when it seems called for?"

*John:* "Not at all, though I suspect that having some notion of the otherness of the divine judgment may sometimes complicate the question of the patient's welfare. For example, those who are trying to puzzle out the dying person's relationship with God may be dealing with more factors than secular people when it comes to such decisions as terminating respirators."

*Deborah:* "Another terrible nest of hard questions and decisions. Even if one removed the legal issues, which often seem to complicate such questions for the wrong reasons—simply to avoid liability to lawsuits and huge financial penalties—the question of terminating life would remain difficult, at least in my view. Still, I am fairly sure that prolonging life by artificial means when there is little chance of normal life returning is unnecessary. I don't see why we have any moral obligation to sustain people who are functional vegetables."

*John:* "Neither do I."

*Deborah:* "I guess, though, that thinking of any human being as finally the 'property' of God does relativize the power of doctors or the state or the person's family to dispose of the person as they find convenient. I guess it would be a strong pressure to consider the person as valuable, even sacred, in some independent or objective way that would make all decisions about the ultimate disposition of the person quite grave."

*John:* "I would hope so, and I suspect that most medical personnel in fact have considerable sensitivity to the rights of the patient that stem from his or her simple humanity, which may be damaged or dysfunctional in terminal cases but still attaches itself to the body of the unconscious person, or even to the person's corpse. I doubt that the incidence of disrespect or abuse of unconscious patients or corpses is high, though of course I don't know."

*Deborah:* "Anything is possible, as the abuse of patients not terminal shows, but I agree with you that abuse is not the general rule. There is respect for the dignity of the patient in most hospitals, and behind that there is an implicit confession that the human being, however disabled, is valuable, even sacred. You see this expressed in heart-wrenching ways when parents and doctors are dealing with little babies who have Down's Syndrome, or even much worse impairments. The first instinct may be to recoil in horror or disgust, because we have a primitive mechanism that makes us reject humanity that is twisted or seriously impaired. But as soon as the little thing cries or moves or does anything even remotely resembling normal infant behavior, a surge of compassion usually comes, often with many tears, and somehow those tears humanize the situation and provide some healing. I'm not much inclined to contrast the virtues of men and women, but I do think that women's easier access to tears has served them well in many painful situations. I do think that having our bodies and spirits conspire to mourn expressively is a great help."

*John:* "Yes, and it's still hard for men, at least in our country, to appreciate such a bodily wisdom and act upon it. Maybe somewhat parallel is the difficulty men, and no doubt many women, have in letting go of their troubles, dropping their need to fight for control. I understand that fighting disease or misfortune has its benefits. I'm not talking about premature surrender or cowardice. I'm talking about dealing with the feelings of being overwhelmed and learning how to lay them down or cast them upon God. In many cases, they have to be picked up again, because there is more fighting to do. But because we have laid them down for a while, and shared the responsibility with God, we can pick them up again with renewed strength. At least, that's been my experience. At the moment I'm dealing with a relative who is in a horrible situation—long-term sickness, worries about money and care of kids, few reasons to think the future will be anything but grim. The tension that long-term suffering brings into a household is frightening to observe. People's nerves fray and soon they are snapping at one another, which of course compounds their frustration and guilt. It is clear that heartfelt prayer is one of the things keeping my relative going. Without that, I think several people in her family might snap."

*Deborah:* "I think that medical personnel are becoming more aware of such factors. We've known instinctively about tension, and for some time there have been studies of the bad effects of stress, but lately I've also heard more about the spiritual aspects of disease and healing. Physicians who ten years ago would have been loath to admit a place for faith or prayer sometimes surprise me nowadays. Perhaps they have just gotten older and seen more cases where patients or families who should have been in despair managed not to be. Whatever the reason, I find the change welcome. It's another confession that we are not God, and so another bit of humility and truth. If recourse to faith and prayer helps people heal or face their deaths well, we ought to welcome it wholeheartedly."

§≈

*John:* "We've been speaking about the injustice of a premature death, and the way that contemplating death forces one to appreciate the limits of human judgments. What about the other sorts of injustice? Consider the differences in the financial and social statuses of the patients in your hospital. Consider the differences in the rewards given doctors, nurses, and maintenance people. And, then, consider the wider social factors in the etiology of disease: poverty, drug usage and sexual activity (for instance, in the spread of AIDS), the economics and politics of abortion, the dispersal of funds for military weapons (funds that might be used to fight cancer, or to educate people to healthier lifestyles), the pollution of the environment and of us human beings along with it. No disease is an island, standing alone. If ecology and process thought (and, for some, Buddhism) have taught us anything, it is the intrinsic connectedness of all things in the universe. You can start with AIDS or abortion or cancer, but if you persist courageously, before long you'll be into economics, politics, and culture at large, including religion. How do you feel about injustice—all that ought not to be—in this wider perspective?"

*Deborah:* "I feel overwhelmed, by both your question and the reality it brings to mind. Medicine, like much of academic life, is highly specialized. Even family practice is now a specialty. We have few people sitting back and contemplating the big picture. Too often we prescind from the social factors in disease and health care alike, though the role of insurance companies, state legislators, and economics generally assures that health care has its feet on the ground. Naturally, I've intuited that a deep injustice runs through the entire fabric of social factors conditioning both disease and health care. I haven't concentrated on that injustice, because I've suspected that concentrating on it would only limit my effectiveness (rage is not conducive to patient, day by day plugging away at one's little corner of the whole picture). But I have been aware of it, and sometimes it's made me cry. I'm ashamed to say that I've cried more because I felt abused personally than because of large-scale wrongs in the system as a whole, but in my defense I might say that I've also intuited that the wrongs done me personally were frequently symptoms of the wider perversions."

*John:* "Yes. Everywhere, it seems, the wrong people are in charge more frequently than not. In national politics, the church, and university life, administration regularly goes to those willing to connive and deal and put their time into bureaucracy. The more creative people, or those most focused on the heart of the enterprise, find administration repulsive, but in refusing to have much to do with it, they cede power to the mediocre. There are exceptions to this rule, of course, and one has to admire the self-spending of intelligent, dedicated administrators. On the whole, though, becoming a bishop, or a dean, or a member of congress is not a move into creativity and exemplary service. Moreover, the need we all feel to justify our existence (which need seems compounded among the mediocre) assures that administrators will arrogate the largest salaries and honors to themselves, while the people doing the work for which the institution was created receive considerably less financial compensation. So the priests who actually staff the parishes, and the teachers who actually staff the classrooms, and the people who actually think up the programs that would move the country forward become humored and patronized, because the money, which interweaves with the power, is in the hands of those who live off such work and pretend to direct it. On occasion, administrators do direct it well, and there are wonderful 'enablers' of fine programs. More often than not, though, we construct and tolerate institutions that put power and financial reward at odds with genuine creativity and service. That is one of the greatest injustices I see, not only because it warps the relations between means and ends, but also because it results in a willful distortion of what the institution in question exists to do, its *raison d'être*. Such a warping and distortion is evil—an index of original sin—and it creates much of the sadness that afflicts citizens everywhere."

*Deborah*: "Original sin, then, is the distortion in basic relations or systems or institutions. It is the disorder that taints the entire atmosphere, poisoning the people and work situated there before they even begin. I don't know that that's especially consoling, but it is illuminating. I've never heard original sin described that way before."

*John*: "It's not my creation. Mainstream theologians have been saying things like that for twenty years. The deeper issue, though, which I love to consider, is what systemic injustice or warping does to the matter of theodicy—the justice of God. God is responsible for the world, in some final assessment, and so God must be accountable for the systematic wrongs in the world. You probably are more interested in getting a handle on limited systematic evils, such as the wrongs that tilt medical care. But I've always been fascinated by the most ultimate considerations, such as how one can put together a good God and a defective creation."

*Deborah:* "Let's take them one at a time, beginning with the more limited disorders. What would you say is the single greatest need of a disordered system such as present-day American health care?"

*John:* "I would say a new vision of how human beings ought to relate to one another—a new sense of our corporate, mutually interdependent character. From such a new vision, we might reintroduce the primacy of the common good and make secondary individual rights, profits, honors, and the other things that both sour people to hard work and ensure that much of their work will misfire. I guess we're back to the question of a communitarian or socialist vision of human existence, and so to the related question of how we might motivate people to work for moderate wages and moderate tokens of power, rather than in the personally ambitious ways our present American systems stimulate. For medicine, that might mean a solid income, sufficient to recompense people for long years of study and demanding work, and to allow them to raise their families in comfort (but not luxury), along with a primary focus on curing the sick—i.e. making the main satisfaction helping people get well. I know that many medical personnel, to their great credit, continue to make that their main motivation, but they swim against the stream inasmuch as the financial rewards, power, and honors often have little to do with direct care of patients. The parallels in academic life would amount to the ways in which good teaching and creative scholarship often play second fiddle to the agenda of administrators, which places athletics, satisfying boosters and local business people, or pandering to students' social lives before the reason to be of any healthy college, which is learning, pure and simple. The parallel in the church would be the many ways in which we have to fight to make serving people the sacraments, nourishing their minds and hearts in faith, helping them bear their trials, and getting them to work hard to transform their pagan society more central than kowtowing to distant authorities or cosying up to secular powers. In each case, a communitarian and radical view of the enterprise might oust the present aggression, ambition, and individualism to very good effect. But the question would remain: Are we good enough, as human beings, to do our medicine, or our academic work, or our ministerial work for the right reasons? Can we muster enough faith in our ideals, our own confessed sense of what really fulfills people, to make money and status and honor and power secondary? How we answer that question says a good deal about our view of human nature."

§∾

*Deborah:* "You mean that if we don't think human beings are capable of the ideals we see are necessary for decent, just institutions, we have no logical reason for hope."

*John:* "Yes, and that unless we find a reason for hope, we won't achieve what justice we might. My reason for hope, perhaps paradoxically, is what God can do to transform human nature. I believe that human beings most essentially are the creatures who can be elevated by God to an honesty, justice, and love that is superhuman. The enigma is that we need such an elevation to become what we ought to be, what we most want to be."

*Deborah:* "That reminds me of Jesus' saying to the effect that certain kinds of evils or demons can be cast out only by prayer and fasting. I would interpret what you've said to mean that unless people bear down hard, really discipline themselves, they will not achieve the creativity or justice they are capable of."

*John:* "I would add that though discipline is necessary, so is surrendering oneself to the larger powers implied by the mysteriousness of the human situation—opening oneself to the help, the grace, of God. Otherwise, one is what theologians call a Pelagian, a person trying to pull himself or herself up by the bootstraps."

*Deborah:* "Let's move now to the other question, about the final justice of God. If God is the creator, why is the world so full of injustice and suffering?"

*John:* "No one can know, of course, in the sense of having a sure explanation. But when I speculate about that question, I find myself confronted with the apparent reality that God's ways clearly are very different from our human ways—as far as the heavens from the earth, as Isaiah says. I don't abandon God, because I've already come to the conclusion or decision that without God there is no hope for meaning or redemption at all. But I do abandon my demands to understand according to my spontaneous, human criteria. I think this is the 'answer' that the book of Job offers us. We simply don't have the scale to understand the universe, and unless we can understand the universe fully, we can't understand how any particular event or fate fits in. Certainly, this seems very cold comfort: God *may* have richer purposes than we can discern. To warm it, I look to the fate of Jesus, who was exemplary in suffering innocently. If God found it necessary to let Jesus, his especially beloved, suffer rejection, torture, and a horrible death, then we are involved with deeper matters than we can comprehend. That's probably what Saint Paul had in mind when he spoke of wrestling with 'principalities and powers.' But the example of Jesus, which fills out when one contemplates his resurrection and sending of the Spirit, says that we can endure, even embrace, what we cannot understand. In an amazing way, God asks us to trust that there is a purpose, that things will be sorted out, that in the end we will understand the necessity of suffering. When Jesus tried to explain his fate to the discouraged disciples on the road to Emmaus, he asked rhetorically: 'Was it not necessary that the Christ suffer?' That necessity is very strange, yet Luke makes it a key factor in his presentation of Jesus. Jesus was moving under the impetus of a divine plan."

*Deborah:* "So you're inclined to give God a *carte blanche?*"

*John:* "I think I have to."

*Deborah:* "But surely you continue to struggle to understand, and surely it bothers you terribly when injustice seems to prosper. If that is so, isn't the blank check you give God a final, maybe even a desperate measure? When all else has failed, you surrender your spirit to God, because 'God' stands for your final hope that existence is not meaningless."

*John:* "I also surrender my spirit to God at the beginning and throughout any venture, if I appreciate the significance of 'God.' The God of the Deists stood apart from the world. Having wound it up like a clock, he was content to listen to its ticking. What I would call a truer God is the very possibility of there continuing to be a world. This God not only brought the world into being, through the Big Bang or whatever else cosmologists can suggest. He or she also lures the world forward, as the comprehensive good and fulfillment that all creatures seek. The real God is the source of being, making things not mere possibilities but actualities. In the depths of each creature, the real God is the final reason for the creature to be, and so the inmost significance that the creature carries. What the psalmist puts poetically—if we fly to the highest heaven, God is there, and if we descend to the lowest depths, God is also there—the Christian metaphysician puts ontologically: all being derives from God."

*Deborah:* "So God is the author of evil—isn't that the conclusion that the atheist would draw?"

*John:* "God is not the author of evil, but it is difficult to say how or why apart from faith. The classical defense of God analyzes evil as non-being—the privation of existence, order, and reason—and so claims that God is not responsible for evil. Concerning human affairs, the defense goes on to say that God has made people free and respects their freedom so completely that he allows them to sin, even to the point of ruining themselves and causing others great pain. The reason God has such respect for human freedom is that freedom is the necessary condition for full love—something that legalists, both inside the church and out, fail to understand. Still, I doubt that this kind of reflection does much for the parent who has just had a child drown, or for the Jew or Gypsy reflecting on a family exterminated by the Nazis. In the crunch, we have to believe that God is greater than the evils we witness, and that somehow God is dealing with them—both holding them in check and assuring that they become the means to a much greater good. I don't understand the divine reasoning behind the crucifixion of Christ, but I do understand the church's instinct that the redemption Christ accomplished is a surpassing sign of God's love. If Christ himself thought it worthwhile to suffer so wretchedly, who am I to question the divine wisdom?"

*Deborah:* "That's a good question. Who is any of us to question the divine wisdom? If it is manifest that we cannot understand the world in which we find ourselves, what ought we to do? Ancient peoples worshiped what they could not understand—the volcano spewing lava, the earth turning green each spring. We moderns find such worship credulous, because we have learned how volcanoes work and why the earth turns green. But such progress has not brought us full understanding. We may know how volcanoes work but we do not understand why there have to be volcanoes—what their 'necessity' is. I can understand opening oneself to the mysteriousness of such a necessity, as long as it does not mean stopping our drive to understand natural, or human, mechanisms and striving to improve people's lives with the knowledge we've gained. Certainly, what we have learned by studying the human body has greatly increased our ability to alleviate its pains."

*John:* "Yes, I agree completely. I would add, though, that the mysteriousness of the human body remains. Why did it evolve as it did? How does it happen that so intricate yet vulnerable an entity comes into being? What is the source and significance of thought, which distinguishes the human body from all other creatures? Those are not questions we will answer in any future that I can foresee, because they are not empirical questions. They call for either an evaluation of significance or a comprehensive grasp of the entire natural order. Evaluations depend on the hierarchy of goods that the evaluator employs. In the case of human thought, for example, how significant is it that thought makes us wonder about and desire eternity? In the case of our trying to get a comprehensive view of all of creation, the mind boggles. Unified field theory, as present-day cosmologists use the term, is far from being a comprehensive understanding of how creation unfolded, let alone why creation began in the first place and why it embraces so much injustice and suffering. For answers to those questions, we have to enter the mind of God—which is why many theologians have spoken of heaven as a beatific vision that would give us a sufficient understanding of God to clarify the rationale of creation."

# 5

# *In Search of Love*

*Deborah:* "I'm surprised that we haven't spoken more about love and what its presence or absence does to faith. My sense is that love is crucial. Certainly in my own life, which is no model, the pursuit of love has been a major preoccupation. Indeed, sometimes I think that I'm divorced and possess so many wrenching memories because I pursued love excessively. I bought a lot of the romance associated with the American dream. I loved more intensely than wisely."

*John:* "The Christians I most admire manage to make all of theology, and all of practical life, a function of love. For example, they make it credible that God's motives in creation were only to fashion beings with whom to share the divine existence lovingly. They show how the career of Christ, culminating in his death and resurrection, was an outgrowth of God's desire to communicate the divine substance, which is love. Jesus crucified is the divine love enfleshed and suffering the onslaughts of what hates love and light. Jesus resurrected is the divine love triumphant—stronger than death, more creative than hatred. From the perspective of the loving God, all of human life is a drama in which God's self-offer is being accepted or rejected."

*Deborah:* "So I should not give up, not stop looking for a relationship that might consume and fulfill me? Part of me wants to think that my tendency to seek a passionate love has been praiseworthy, but another part looks at the scars it's brought and brands it foolish. I don't know whether you can understand the message that I received as a teenager, growing up in a small town in the midwest and going off to nursing school on the west coast. *The* measure of my success would be the marital relationship I achieved—the way I welded my destiny to that of a good man. The orgasmic character of the message had much to do with sex, but it had more to do with a woman's supposed nature. A man without a woman was like a ship without a sail, but there was nothing worse in this universe than a woman without a man—that's how the popular music portrayed it. I was quite bright and independent, but that did not keep me from thinking that my greatest delight and achievement ought to be snaring a very desirable man and, by deliciously subtle indirections, getting him to desire and admire me so greatly that he'd do whatever I wanted. The result of this propaganda, which probably merely transposed into a new key the message broadcast to most women throughout history, is a generation of women whose subtlety of social intelligence still fascinates me. The other day I was at a lecture by a Nobel Laureate. The upper crust of the city had been at a black tie dinner for him the night before. Before the lecture I heard one woman say to another, 'Oh, you were at the banquet last night. How was it? What did you wear?' That put it in a nutshell. 'What did you wear' meant 'How did you feel? What was the romantic temperature in the room? Who saw you, and whom did you see, and what did you intuit about the social relations, the shifts of status, crackling throughout the crowd?' It was so brilliant a condensation of the significance of high-art-come-to-town, and so pathetic, that I could only sigh in familiar amazement."

*John:* "Well, if we could say that the real significance of such highly refined social awareness and romanticism is the search for a love both dramatic and demanding, we might redeem many of such otherwise damnable times. The dramatic aspect seems easy enough to verify. Most people find sexual attraction, or even absorbing friendship, so exciting that they are stirred by the slightest hint of it. The demanding aspect is more problematic: how much is dalliance, and how much the desire for an attraction, a self-validation, that would require the best of us and purify our souls?"

*Deborah:* "You're talking to a prime-time dramatiste, you know, and you'll have to take it from her that the demanding aspect is usually present. I want a love that will change and consume me. In another age, I might have conceived of that love as my becoming a missionary to a foreign land, or my becoming the Lady Fair of a chivalrous knight, exalted to the heavens and required to possess the strictest purity. In our culture, the obvious imagery is of a romantic passion that brings fulfillment and wisdom, with just enough suffering to make it exceptional— worthy of prime time, not just the soaps. I don't know how to evaluate the attraction of grand passion. I can step back and mock it, yet it has been very influential in my life. At times I've been so hungry for an absorbing relationship, something that might devour me body and soul, that it's been like water on the brain, upsetting my balance. That may not be typical of American women, let alone of American men, but I don't feel that I'm alone. There's a brisk business in schlocky books about women who love too much, about smart women who make dumb choices. Their dumb choices, you can be sure, are not about their wardrobes, or their cars, or even their jobs. Their dumb choices are about men. No matter what their IQs or educations, they seem to throw out reason, abandon all common sense, when it comes to affairs of the heart. You're a man with some intuition. You must be aware of all this. How does it strike you?"

*John:* "Oh, I'm not sure I want to get into those waters. That's risky business."

*Deborah:* "Coward. I'm serious. Ninety percent of the romantic energy I'm talking about, of the first connotation of 'love' that comes to mind, is heterosexual. Men don't hold up their share of the burdens that love imposes, including the burden of analyzing it so as to lessen tragic mistakes. Thinking about love has become women's work, in a way that has injured both sexes. Because women's work is not valued, love has not been valued as it ought to be. Because women's reflections on love have tended to go round and round, powered by an emotion with limited outlets, while men's reflections have been pathetic attempts at 'objectivity,' we've all missed the union of light and warmth we've been seeking, sometimes desperately. It's time that men did their share, and that men and women came together and spoke more honestly about something so crucial to their mutual welfare."

*John:* "What can I say? You're right, but that doesn't give me much confidence. I'd love to talk with women about love, but if we have to personalize it I'm afraid it would be embarrassing."

*Deborah:* "Men! Of course we have to personalize it. It's not real otherwise. And so it might be embarrassing—so what? Isn't embarrassment a small price to pay for enlightenment? Besides, there are ways of speaking about personal, even intimate experiences, that work by allusion and implication more than direct statement and so lessen embarrassment. One doesn't have to be crude or graphic. Take the matter of emotional need. Don't you think people should talk more about their hunger for soul-satisfying friendships, or for loves that nourish their entire selves, bodies and spirits? Don't you think theologians should make that a prime topic. Love makes the world go round. People who need people are the luckiest people in the world. The song titles are banal, but the reality they wrestle with is the stuff of life. Indeed, more often than not the people who are turned off by the songs are unhappy in their own loves and so can't stand being reminded of what they once hoped for."

*John:* "I can see that this is a topic warming the cockles of your heart. Theologians have had trouble with it, because they've felt bound to make the love of God, *agape,* very different from human loves full of desire (*eros*). I sense that this distinction has begun to break down, because I've seen several good books dealing with the desire God has for us human beings, the passion and longing. The biblical motif of the marriage between the Lord and Israel, or between Christ and the church, may be coming back into vogue. Once there were splendid commentaries on the Song of Song that used it to explore the byplay between God and the human spirit. I hope we see new ones before long. But you are more interested in human passions, and theologians have been reluctant to make love between the sexes a prime analogy for the nature of God."

§

*Deborah:* "I think one of the things that has most put me off about religion has been its prudishness. I know that some eastern religions are full of sex, and that the western religions are full of gore, but in my time the American churches and synagogues have not been places where human passion got much blessing. Yet passion is what brings us alive. Sure, we also need sweet reason, sagacious repose, but unless we're steamed up about people and causes we're only living and partly living, as Eliot put it. I can't understand why the churches are so afraid of passion, when their God is a consuming fire and their Christ was a blazing prophet. It's as though the bean counters put on miters and took over the chanceries."

*John:* "Well, the history of 'enthusiasm,' as theologians have tended to call passionate, charismatic movements, shows them to have been a mixed blessing. More times than not they have blazed out of control, turning heretical and dividing the church. It's a tough question: how to balance prudence and fierce commitment. What is wisdom and what is dessication? I go back and forth, hoping to find instances of the balance, the strong love and solid judgment, that I associate with the great saints."

*Deborah:* "I guess my own pains show the need for solid judgment, but I'd rather be in pain than be without feeling. And, I think that most of our genuine wisdom about people only comes from considerable pain. The people who risk little learn little. The people who try hard to create deep, transforming relationships at least have the satisfaction of realizing how difficult such ventures are. If I were to take religion seriously, I'd have to take the same approach to God. God would have to become the love of my life."

*John:* "That's excellent theology. The Jesus of revelation says that it's better to be hot or cold than lukewarm. The lukewarm get vomited from his mouth. The cold, presumably, are the doubters of God, and the notion seems to be that they can be turned around. Something is going on in them. God stirs them up. With time, their passionate negativity may become positive—perhaps by their realizing that most of what they were told about God was false. The hot may become problems to the authorities, but they keep alive in the church and the world the heart of the religious and human matter. As Deuteronomy put it, the call sounding deep in the human heart is to love the Lord, our God, with whole mind, heart, soul, and strength. Perhaps your longing to love unrestrictedly is really a longing for God."

*Deborah:* "That's too quick and clever by half. My longing

has been embodied, emphatically. I want a lover I can cling to, body and spirit. God is too remote, too abstract, too ethereal. My world focuses on eyes and mouths, on food and drink. I love the earth, its colors and sounds. I love the body, its pleasures and revelations. If I could redo my life, I'd be an artist, maybe a musician, so that I could focus my intelligence more sensuously."

*John:* "But surely the pleasures of the body cannot be divorced from the pleasures of the spirit, just as the pains of the body beleaguer the mind. And the revelations of the body, don't they galvanize the mind, make it seek correlations and generalizations? I doubt that you're as sensual or sensuous as you proclaim. If it's eyes that attract you, it has to be because they are the window of the soul. If it's the mouth, it must be not only for kisses but also for words of wit and comfort. There is no great excitement in the body alone. It's when the body becomes sacramental, a symbolic revelation of holy meanings, that the body becomes riveting. It's when beauty, grace, strength, pleasure, and the rest elevate our minds and hearts that we feel being human is a blessed thing."

*Deborah:* "O.K., so I misspoke, or overspoke, myself. The politicians do it every day. I agree that the excitement comes when there's a union of thought and feeling. I agree that music is wonderful because it makes wit and play sonorous. But that doesn't remove my problems with most churches, because it remains true that they are not harbors of sensuous beauty, that they do not make the gospel something to tingle the nerves and joints."

*John:* "Perhaps so. Much of that is in the eye or body of the beholder, but I agree that it's been some time since I came away from church thrilled. On the other hand, the churches have, perforce, to deal with people's sufferings, which can dampen the message of joy, and they have to deal with a great range of temperaments, most of which are less passionate than yours. I don't think any of that absolves the churches of the sins of torpor and timidity, but it does beg a passionaria like yourself for patience."

*Deborah:* "Patience! My father used to talk about patience. The other day I found myself talking to Renée about patience and I burst out laughing. I suppose it is something that comes into focus in middle age. But I still resent its being dragged in to dampen enthusiasm and slow action. I still find it the dodge of the do-nothings, the brake of the faint-hearted."

*John:* " 'In patience you will possess your souls'—that just popped into my brain. I think it's from one of the epistles of Peter. But it probably has more to do with suffering than with gravity or prudence or slowing things down. Peter is saying that the hardships of life, of clinging to faith, will work a purification. He is saying that if people can endure, they will find a splendid meaning. No doubt for him this was tied up with the resurrection of Christ, which he expected to share. But it remains a formidable statement about our spiritual condition. You quoted T.S. Eliot a few minutes ago. One of the things that gives his poetry such depth is its rumination about suffering. In great action, there is greater passion. We undergo more than we control. We die more certainly than we live. And unless we come to grips with such passion, we have the experience but miss the meaning."

*Deborah:* "Perhaps so, but I can't believe that the passion we ought to be appreciating isn't heartfelt, emotional, something that brings us to the center of ourselves, or even outside of ourselves. Certainly the sufferings that love brings, including the times that one has to wait, to endure, to be 'patient' and let happen what will, can be soul-searing. I'm opposed only to the implication that we should sit back and become spectators at our own lives. I think that's dead-wrong—a prescription for dying twenty years before they lower you into the grave."

*John:* "Well, I like dealing with spitfires—it's very interest-

ing. But I observe that God seems to have created many phleg-
matic types, who must have some rights, and that in the spiritual
life, where one is trying to find God, there are seasons of fire
and seasons of ice. Sometimes God seems far away and one's
sins are depressing. Sometimes God seems very near and grace
abounds. We can shape the tempo and pattern a little bit, by
being faithful or faithless, but most of it is out of our hands. The
mysteriousness is constant, but whether it seems personal and
loving or impersonal and indifferent varies greatly. The utility of
the Song of Songs includes its poetic rendering of the seasons of
intimacy. It puts more romantically the lesson of Ecclesiastes
that for everything there is a season, and for every time a purpose under heaven. 'Under heaven' means that we can't understand such purposes and seasons—that we have to possess our
souls in patient trust."

*Deborah:* "There you go again, turning mystical. I wonder,
though, about my impatience with the spiritual. It may be, as
you suggested when talking about the cold, that I have been
given a bad understanding of God. If God could be considered a
lover who comes and goes, whose rhythms interweave with my
rhythms of body and spirit, I might reconsider prayer. You
asked me at the beginning of this recent series of talks why I
don't pray. I think much of the reason is that I've never felt
there was anyone at the other end, listening and being moved."

ॐ

*John:* "Well, certainly God doesn't answer the way a human interlocutor does, but many people report that their prayer
is not just talking to themselves. In the measure that they pour
out their hearts and ask the divine mysteriousness to help, or
accept, or support them, they come away relieved. Others, of
course, speak very personally to Christ or Mary or one of the
saints. They imagine Christ as he was when he walked among

the sick or preached to the crowds, and by making themselves contemporary to those events they achieve a sort of communion with Christ. Psychologists might say that they are only fantasizing, but they themselves can feel more is going on. As long as the intentionality of prayer, its 'direction,' is outward, toward a divinity considered independent of the self, what happens because of prayer, the shifts of mentality or feeling that occur, can be believed to be the workings of the divine Spirit."

*Deborah:* "I don't deny that many pious people make that sort of report, but it doesn't move me very much. The most I can speak of, from my own life, is finding that an intense experience, whether in personal exchanges or in moments like that one I had by the river, takes me beyond my usual, secular sense of things and inserts me into a great mysteriousness."

*John:* "Suppose you were to linger with that mysteriousness. Suppose its beauty or grandeur or incomprehensibility were to warm your heart, to make you feel that having been made a human being is a marvelous fate, something for which to give profound thanks. Would that strike you as incongruous, or repugnant, or antagonistic to deep convictions you hold?"

*Deborah:* "I've never thought about such a question. Off the top of my head, the answer is that, if such actions or feelings or thoughts came naturally, were not forced or 'pious,' I would have no problem with them. Indeed, I would be happy to have them. I'm not opposed to deep feelings, or even to awe or humility in face of the mysteriousness of human existence. Certainly, I'm not opposed to gratitude for the good things in life or love for all that's beautiful. Inasmuch as those might be religious responses, I'm not opposed to being religious. I'm just opposed to making things up, to being pressured to think or feel in prefabricated ways, because of a supposed faith. If 'God' were to emerge in my life naturally, spontaneously, as something or someone I found myself dealing with honestly, or necessarily, I would have no objection. I doubt that that would send me

running to church, but it would probably make me more interested in what religious people think God really is."

*John:* "What do you think God really is?"

*Deborah:* "I don't think that I'm a religious person, but in
my experience 'God' is the name we give to what's best in existence—what gives us our ideals and keeps us going. We have a
sense of justice, a hunger for love, minds that want to be
flooded with light. I associate 'God' with these built-in human
qualities. God would have to be more objective than just our
human needs, but I think that God makes most sense when he
or she is correlated with our human needs. In my own case,
'God' might stand for the perfect lover. He would have none of
the limitations of human lovers. He would understand me completely and bring out the best in me. I could trust him entirely,
and the joy of my life would be to live united with him."

*John:* "The old writers on prayer sometimes said that all
human souls are feminine, regardless of the bodies they inform.
Such writers went on to say that any Christian's prayer can have
the motif of espousal and marriage, regardless of the person's
sex. God is the lover and the human person is the beloved. The
relationship can be likened to a human betrothal, perhaps with
symbolic help from the Song of Songs. Nowadays, many theologians want to bring out the stereotypically feminine attributes
of God. God continues to transcend sex, but if one is to deal
with God through a personification that attributes sexual characteristics, those characteristics should be a balance of what we
tend to think of as male and what we tend to think of as female.
That raises an interesting line of questioning. First, should men
start to think of their relation with God on the model of a love
affair in which God could be the female partner, beautiful and
beguiling? Second, have women been more prayerful through
the ages (as general stereotyping suggests) because it has been
easier for women to relate to God as a lover than it has been for
men (God generally being thought of as male)? I don't know

how one would answer such questions, but they suggest that future explorations of prayer could be very interesting. If we say that prayer, as the epitome of a personal faith, ought to be primarily a love affair, then cultural shifts in our senses of the sexes are bound to make a considerable impact on our prayer."

*Deborah:* "So it would be fine for me to think of God as the best of men (and of course much more) and regard my dealings with the divine mysteriousness as a passionate love affair?"

*John:* "Why not? So long as you did not deny the ways in which God may be impersonal (the force creating and running the natural world), and in which God may be feminine, you shouldn't get into any troubles with orthodoxy. You also have to consider, of course, that no human language captures God, so 'God' is beyond all our talk about the divine masculinity or femininity or impersonality. Whatever we say about God, no matter how true, God is more unlike than like—because God is infinite, and we are finite. Granted all this, however, you can deal with God as though he were the best of male lovers. Many ardent female saints have."

*Deborah:* "But most of them have focused on Christ. Do I have to focus on Christ as well?"

*John:* "You're getting us into the knotted question of how to revise traditional language. Traditionally, the Christian God has been considered a masculine Trinity. The Father is the originator, the Son is the originated, and the Spirit is the result of their love. Some of the biblical imagery for the Spirit is feminine, but on the whole the traditional Christian imagery for the Trinity is masculine. So, you can relate to any of the three divine persons (who of course are not distinct individuals the way human persons have to be) as to a male personality, but you don't have to. As well, you can relate to Christ as to a male, which he was historically, and much in Christian tradition urges you to pray to Christ, who is the Son incarnate, but you don't have to. You can pray to the God reflected in the seas or the mountains or the skies or the earth. You can pray to God as the feminine force that moved over the waters of creation and brings forth the great proliferation of creatures. So long as you don't insist that any one of these images (or the collectivity of them, for that matter) sums up the divine being, you can relate to God however you feel moved to do. One day you can relate one way, another day another way. It is the same God, too rich for any of our depositories to handle."

*Deborah:* "And all of this is legitimate, orthodox? I would have thought that Christian theology would impose more restrictions. This sounds like a free-wheeling or free-association suggested by humanistic psychology."

*John:* "There is great freedom in Christian spirituality. Not all Christians are aware of the diversity of their traditions, and not all are strong enough to make use of what Paul called 'the freedom for which Christ has set us free,' but in itself Christian faith is a great writ of emancipation. Those who serve the true, living God have no human masters, including their own superegos. They are called out of the bondages that keep most of their contemporaries chained to worldly values and bound to be disappointed. In love and truth and creativity, they can find the world made fresh each day. 'Behold, I make all things new,' the apocalyptic Christ proclaims. Those who have ears to hear his message find the world and themselves much changed. There are more things under the sun than the textbooks and pundits realize. There are many fewer dead-ends and many more new beginnings."

৯৯

*Deborah:* "That's a comforting thought. I suppose that much of how we evaluate our situation at a given time depends on our sense of whether it is a dead-end or might lead on to something more satisfying. We human beings do have a need to keep growing. I see that every week in dealing with elderly people, as well as children. The elderly people who do best are those who keep busy, who never run out of things they're curious about, things they'd still like to try. The children who do worst are those who have been dulled by inattention. Children don't thrive unless someone takes an interest in them, and much of children's thriving boils down to their wanting to understand the world around them. If a kid has strong interests, things he or she wants to learn about, other things usually fall into place."

*John:* "So, what does the elderly Deborah White, or the kid Debbie White, want to learn about? What does she still want to try?"

*Deborah:* "I still want to read good books, and listen to good music, and travel to new countries. I still want to eat good food and drink good wine. I still want to improve my office, make it more efficient so that it serves our patients better. Most of all, though, I still want an absorbing personal relationship, one that will put a bounce in my step and provoke me to find the world a more beautiful place."

*John:* "I suppose one way to think about people's mental health is to find out whether they have strong interests that keep them growing, and to evaluate how worthy such interests are. I know people who are passionate about improving their putting, and I know many more who have invested a great deal of themselves in the stock market. If those interests keep them growing, it's hard to criticize them. But I wonder about the significance of becoming the best putter at the country club, or the significance of adding another hundred thousand dollars to one's estate. What are the interests that nourish the soul? What is the growth that takes us toward the maturity, the selfhood, that we most deeply want and that is best for us?"

*Deborah:* "Those are the kinds of questions I should be asking you. You're the theologian. On the other hand, I guess those are the kinds of questions I should be asking myself. Sometimes I have asked them, of course. In my own words, my own thoughts, I have wondered about what is really important, what I ought to stress. Some of the books I've read, along with common sense and common observation, have convinced me that Freud was right. People who can love and work successfully are mentally healthy. Love and work focus our greatest needs, our best capacities. So I have tried to make my work significant. Sometimes I get depressed and wonder whether I haven't made a bad choice. Sometimes the bureaucracy is discouraging, and the fact that people keep dying, no matter what anyone does, casts a dark shadow. But more days than not I'm content. I'm not going to win a Nobel Prize for great discoveries in science, but I don't have to blush when people ask me what I do. Growth in my work comes from learning more about how a hospital functions, getting my department better organized, and, above all, slowly clarifying just what it is that we can offer patients, just how we can best relieve their sufferings or buoy up their hopes. As far as love is concerned, I have been even more involved, sometimes to the point of obsession. The presence of love has been my greatest joy and the absence of love has been my heaviest burden. I've made sacrifices for love, and I've made mistakes in love, but the vitality it's brought me, the revelations and pleasures and challenges, has made it worthwhile. I owe my daughter to love, and she has become a central focus of my life. I can't conceive of my life without her, she's made so much difference. Watching her grow has been a delight, as well as a worry, and now that she's on the verge of leaving home, I feel an amazing mixture of both pride and sadness. We're both on the verge of a new phase in our lives."

*John:* "I would add to Freud's two needs two more, prayer and politics. I feel more strongly about prayer than politics, but many religious people whom I respect feel just the reverse, so I think both deserve thorough consideration. We've talked enough about prayer for you to know that I think of it as the activity that most directly involves us with God, the divine mysteriousness that Christians explicate in terms of the Trinity and Christ. We've talked enough about work and love for you to know that I agree with you about their significance. By 'politics' I mean playing one's civic roles responsibly, trying to shape the common culture so that it serves the common good. That means informing oneself and voting. It means doing what one can, as one's resources, time, and talents allow, to shape governmental policy, local or national. It means supporting the organizations that help the homeless, the unwed mothers, the alcoholics, the poor, the mentally ill—the entire roster of people down and out. I think that a fully admirable life requires some such political component, just as I think that a fully mature life certainly requires contemplative thoughtfulness and probably requires genuine prayer."

*Deborah:* "Do you see these four activities as separate, or do they overlap? What is the political value of work such as mine, or of your work as a writer? What is the relation between the deep reflection I've put into love affairs and genuine prayer?"

*John:* "I think it's useful to distinguish the four, but that they overlap a great deal. It's useful to distinguish them, because none is exactly the same as any other and each suggests a distinctive challenge. But they overlap a great deal because how we relate to nature, society, our selves, and God comes from a single source, our personal humanity. So, I do think there's a political dimension to your work, and that your work contributes quite directly to making the world a better place. Certainly it contributes more directly than my work as a writer. Setting a broken arm is much more certainly useful than writing an article. I also think that there's an overlap between deep reflection and prayer, precisely because both take us into the mysteriousness I consider divine. The difference between reflection and prayer is the direct address of God that prayer implies. Prayer is personal in ways that reflection or meditation is not. Prayer seeks an interpersonal bond with God, a dialogue. And prayer is only consummated in love, the union of mind and heart with God that makes for a sharing of selves—God's with us, and ours with God."

*Deborah:* "By those criteria, I may be more religious, or at least doing better at the general task of growing toward human maturity, than I thought. I'm still not sure what I think about God, or about Christ, or about the church. I have no clear convictions about immortality, and I don't agree with religious people on many ethical issues (though I guess religious people often don't agree with one another). But our talks do make me question my secularism, and the secularism of many of my friends or colleagues who seem to have dismissed religion as irrelevant. I want a life that is three-dimensional. I'm sure that money and success are not enough. What would be enough, I'm not sure. Sometimes I envy the poets and artists, who seem to have work that is three-dimensional by definition. I suppose in reality they have their own struggles, but trying to create something beautiful, or discover fresh harmonies, is an undertaking so spiritual that it would seem to be its own reward. I'd like to get to the point where I spent most of my time doing things that were their own reward: learning new significant things, making something beautiful and nourishing, helping other people improve their lives. That would be wonderful. If it would also be religious, so much the better, because then religion would be the depth of my humanity. Maybe one day it will be."